The Eleventh Draft

The Eleventh Draft

**CRAFT AND THE WRITING LIFE FROM THE
IOWA WRITERS' WORKSHOP**

edited by
Frank Conroy

HarperCollins*Publishers*

Grateful acknowledgment is given to Alfred A. Knopf, Inc., for permission to reprint exerpts from *The Stories of John Cheever* copyright © 1985 John Cheever.

Excerpts from *A Passage to India* by E. M. Forster, copyright © 1924 by Harcourt, Inc., and renewed 1952 by E. M. Forster, reprinted by permission of the publisher.

HarperCollins books may be purchased for educational, business, or sales promotional use. For information please write: Special Markets Department, HarperCollins Publishers, Inc., 10 East 53rd Street, New York, NY 10022.

FIRST EDITION

Designed by William Ruoto

Library of Congress Cataloging-in-Publication Data

Eleventh draft : craft and the writing life from Iowa Writers'
  Workshop / edited by Frank Conroy. — 1st ed.
      p. cm.
    ISBN 0-06-273639-6
    1. Authorship. 2. Creative writing—Study and teaching (Higher)—
Iowa—History—20th century. 3. Iowa Writers' Workshop.
  I. Conroy, Frank, 1936– . II. Iowa Writers' Workshop.
  III. Title: 11th draft.
PN187.E44 1999
808'.02—dc21   99-28758
                                                          CIP

99 00 01 02 03 ❖/RRD 10 9 8 7 6 5 4 3 2 1

*To Connie Brothers—the heart and soul of the Workshop.
All of us are very deeply in her debt.*

Contents

Acknowledgments

Thanks to Maggie Lee Conroy for her help in matters both technical and literary. Also to Neil Olson for his good offices, and to Jay Papasan, whose idea this was in the first place.

Introduction

All the contributors to this book were once students at the Iowa Writers' Workshop, members of the faculty, or both. All write prose rather than poetry. (Poetry deserves its own book.) My instructions to them were deliberately vague—they were to write about writing, any aspect or approach that caught their fancy. Leaving it open seemed to me to heighten the chances of getting the strongest and least predictable work. And so it was. They came at it from different angles, using different techniques, and each piece is unique. Perhaps the only common tacit assumption is that writing is difficult.

Unlike many activities, say, skiing, for instance, which starts out difficult and becomes easier the more you do it, writing for most artists is fairly easy at first and becomes harder. That is because in the beginning one is carried along by a kind of unconscious mimesis of all that one has read, an exhilarating plunge into techniques, conventions, strategies, and so on, that one has learned more or less by ear, without thinking about them. The discovered ability to create fictive reality on the page, to make characters who seem "real," to feel the mysterious forward thrust of narrative drive—these are intoxicating experiences of great power. The writer simply wants to be in that zone and doesn't spend much time worrying about what the zone actually is.

But rather quickly, as he or she begins to try to "make it new" (in the words of Ezra Pound), the writer is pulled into a deeper consideration of the functioning of written language. As the artist attacks more and more complex and ambitious material while at the same time fine-tuning the language to higher and more precise levels of expressiveness, the entire enterprise slows down, gets harder, and requires greater concentration. Eventually it is no longer enough to simply write within the given traditions of literature (which I call mimesis), but to try to extend or extrapolate that reality by creating something that is new—that is more new, you might say, than it is old. Once a writer has done that, there is no turning back, no matter what the pain and what the pleasure.

It's a hard life because one is dependent on forces that are not fully understood and usually impossible to control. It's scary, because most writers in the midst of making a novel or a short story don't really know if their work is bad or good. Most of them operate on faith. Many of them, having completed a strong piece of work, are not confident they can ever do it again. These fears, and others, are in fact commonplace, and one of the immediate benefits of joining a community of writers is precisely that discovery. Everybody is scared, everyone approaches the empty page with a mixture of dread and hope, and knowing this helps. Simple discoveries lead to more complex discoveries. One learns to be less afraid of the mystical or Zen aspects of the creative process. One learns that a certain amount of uncomfortableness simply comes with the territory.

I've been at the Iowa Writers' Workshop for twelve years and any number of things have become clear. You cannot make a silk purse from a sow's ear. Some will fail. The students—who are an elite bunch to say the least, since we can only admit four percent of those who apply—learn more from each other than they do from the faculty. Two years of reading, of reading each other, and of talking seriously about writing can lead to very fast progress for some and slow progress for others, and there is no way to tell who'll be fast and who'll be slow. Writing is a test of character as well as a test of talent, and talent is more common than character. Oh, I've learned a lot of things, and it has been a privilege to be here, a very, very lucky turning in my life.

These essays are written by people who struggle with both the visible and invisible realities of language every day of their lives, and to whom nothing is more important. Their thoughts and observations are invaluable. Listen up.

—Frank Conroy
July 1999

T. CORAGHESSAN BOYLE

This Monkey, My Back

For a long while there, I was a young writer, and then, for nearly as long, I was a *younger* writer (younger than whom, I used to wonder—Robert Frost?). Now I'm just a writer. Certainly not an old writer, no *eminence gris*, no member of the Academy with yellowed hairs growing out of my ears and nostrils, but a writer, I like to think, of wisdom and maturity, with a few good years left ahead of me. Still, I had a shock a couple of months ago, when an old friend stopped by on his way back from Mexico and revealed something to me about the age we'd attained—or were rapidly approaching. We were sitting at the kitchen table, and he'd just fanned out a group of photographs and narrated the story of each one: I saw the Zócalo, the soap-powder beaches of Puerto Escondido, the catacombs beneath some ancient church. There was a pause, and then he said, "You know, in a couple of years I'm thinking of retiring." I was stunned. This was a vigorous man of forty-nine, a snappy dresser who'd made good money in his own business. "Retire?" I gasped, summoning up ghosts in carpet slippers hunkered before the TV at eleven A.M. and slurping up lime Jell-O and bourbon. All I could think to do was fish through the glossy photos before me till I found the one of the catacombs, shrunken tanned hides and lipless teeth, the claws that used to be fingers, people laid out on slabs like fallen trees. I held it up. "This is my retirement," I told him.

James Baldwin said that we write to give order and structure to a chaotic world, and this is surely part of it, maybe the biggest part, but there's more to it than that. Writing is a habit, an addiction, as powerful and overmastering an urge as putting a bottle to your lips or a spike in your arm. Call it the impulse to make something out of nothing, call it an obsessive-compulsive disorder, call it logorrhea. Have you been in a bookstore lately? Have you seen what these authors are doing, the mountainous piles of the flakes of themselves they're leaving behind, like the neatly labeled jars of shit, piss, and toenail clippings one of Vonnegut's characters bequeathed to his wife, the ultimate expression of his deepest self? Retire? Retire from *that*? Sure, we'll all retire, all of us, once they drain our blood and pump the embalming fluid in.

Unlike most of my compatriots at the Iowa Writers' Workshop in the Seventies, and the major part of my own students now, I didn't develop my addiction in the womb or drink it up with my mother's milk. I wasn't touched by an angel, I didn't wear bottle lenses and braces and hide out in dark corners, my only friend the book, nor was I a Borgesian mole burrowing through my father's library (for the record, my father didn't have a library and never read a book in his life, aside from what might have been forced down his throat at St. Joseph's Home, the Catholic orphanage where he was raised and educated as far as the eighth grade). No, I was a kid like any other kid. I played ball; wandered the vestigial woods of suburban Westchester, killing things; held my own in school, though it was like penal servitude. I was a good kid, I tried to please—as the children of alcoholics so often do—and yet somehow, at fifteen or sixteen, I metamorphosed into a wise guy. A punk. A cynic. A know-it-all. Partly, books were to blame—but not fully, not quite yet. The people I ran with—kids, that is—were the children of educated parents, middle-class and even wealthy parents, and they were sly, smart, and disaffected. Later there would be drugs, but at first there was only desperate-to-get-laid maniacal driving, the usual acts of vandalism, liberated booze— and somehow, miraculously, books. We were proto-hippies, but we didn't know it. We just knew we were caught somewhere between the hoods and the honor students, and that we had a taste for Aldous Huxley, George Orwell, J.D. Salinger, Jack Kerouac. Writing? Never heard of it.

At seventeen, I found myself in Potsdam, New York, at SUNY Potsdam, formerly a normal school, now still heavily teacher-oriented but leaning toward the liberal arts. And music. I went there because I played saxophone and wanted to be a musician and because my academic record to this point slid down the scale from mediocre to hopelessly mediocre and nobody else would take me, even if I'd applied, which I didn't. So there I was, in the frozen skullcap of the world, with my saxophone and my sheet music and little talent and no discipline. I flunked my audition and became a history major. Why history? I didn't know at the time, or I couldn't have defined it, but it had to do with writing. I didn't yet realize it, but I could write, and in history—unlike, say, biology or math—what you did was write essays. I found my first mentor there, in the history department—Dr. Vincent Knapp, who himself had made his way up, hand over hand, from the depths of the working class. He saw something in me—in my writing and my intelligence—and he tried to promote and encourage it. He was the second of my fathers, and I hurt him in the way of Alan Sillitoe's long-distance runner and *his* father/mentor. I didn't attend classes. I hung out with the losers.

But I read. I was introduced to Flannery O'Connor in a sophomore literature class and felt a blast of recognition, and outside class, in the bars and in the company of a small cadre of people like me, I began to read Updike and Bellow and Camus, then Barth, Beckett, Genet, and Gide, as well as Ibsen, O'Neill, Sartre, and Waugh. The library was new, and it smelled of the formaldehyde in the carpets, and the books were new, the ones I was reading, anyway, and they smelled the way books still smell today, of glue and type and paper mills, a smell I grew to associate with pleasure—and with knowledge. After all, as a budding or even an enduring wise guy, I could be even wiser, more cynical, more sardonic and knowing, if I actually knew something.

There was rock and roll, of course, which obliterated my early jazz leanings and made me a student of electrified rage (and which later led to the drums, more saxophone, and finally a kind of unmodulated howling into the microphone to the coordinated thrash of everything else), and then I began taking literature courses and discovered my next mentor, Kelsey B. Harder. Kelsey was chairman of the English Department, and he recognized in me the same talent for writing that had attracted Dr. Knapp over in history. I wounded him, too, with the weapons of indifference and alienation, but I wrote some essays for him and began to feel that there was at least something I could do and do well. I was a junior when I took my first course in creative writing, under the last of my undergraduate tutors, Krishna Vaid.

Krishna is a Harvard-educated Hindu novelist, much enamored of James Joyce, and he had a cultivated, continental air about him. The class mystified me. There were eleven people in it, all of whom were poets, and they were writing poetry that to me, at least, was incomprehensible. (Poetry and I had collided disastrously in high school, when a pompous prig of a teacher read aloud the great poems of English and American literature in a voice so saturated with piety I wanted to set his hair afire, exhume the dead poets, and put them and their books on a slow barge for Patagonia.) Workshops in those days were still evolving and the conduct of Krishna's class was fairly elementary. He would ask a few students to write something for the following week, at which time they would read the result aloud while the rest of us sat in mortified and uncomprehending silence, preparatory to saying absolutely nothing about it. This went on for several weeks before Krishna turned to me and said, "Tom, why don't you put up something next?"

All right, why not? This *was* a writing class, after all, and if I'd been selected for it, I must have been a writer of some sort. Problem was, I'd never actually written anything—other than classroom essays, that is, and now I was confronted with the problem of coming up with something creative, be it a short story, a poem, or (wait a minute) a *play*. We'd been reading the absurdist playwrights in another class, one I attended sporadically and failed miserably, but which featured amazing material in the required texts: "The Bald Soprano"; "Waiting for Godot"; "Rhinoceros"; "The Balcony." I was attracted to these works in particular because it was readily apparent that their authors were wise guys just like me—albeit very sophisticated, very nasty, and very funny wise guys. I wrote a one-act play. Ten or twelve pages. It was called "The Foot," and it dealt with a couple grieving over the loss of their child to the jaws of an alligator; all that remained of him was his left foot, dressed in a tennis shoe, and set in the middle of the coffee table like a holiday centerpiece.

I should say that Krishna—Dr. Vaid—had a face of stone. He never showed the slightest glimmer of joy, transport, hate, hope, disgust, boredom, or mental affliction while my fellow students read out their convoluted and baffling poems. And so, when he nodded to me and I began to read my play aloud, I knew—or thought I knew—what to expect. What ensued was one of the sweet surprises of my life. Krishna began to smile and then to grin and chuckle and finally to laugh without constraint. Grudgingly, my fellow students (who, like me, were the lame and halt of the campus, bearing all sorts of scars both visible and invisible and who were unanimous in their contempt for one another and by extension one another's work) began to drop a sotto voce chuckle here and there. When I finished, flushed with the sort of exhilaration that only comes from driving the ball over the net and directly into your opponent's face, Krishna began to applaud, and so too, though it killed them, did my fellow students. That was it. That was all it took. I was hooked.

Examine the elements involved in this essential scene I've just described for you—visible triumph and public adulation, the trumping of one's competitors, the humble acceptance of the laurel wreath, and the promise of dizzying triumphs to come. It was heady, heady indeed, and it would be usual to say that I never looked back, that I educated myself, worked diligently to develop my talent, and flew like a great stinking harpy eagle to the very heights of Parnassus, but that wouldn't be accurate. I became hooked, it's true, but the drug I craved required dedication, required work, and I soon found other drugs that required nothing more than an open mouth or a trembling blue vein to receive them. Oh, I wrote some short stories in the way I might have taken the clothes to the cleaner's or mowed the lawn for my father (who sat in his Barcalounger cradling his drink as if it were about to explode), but I didn't feel any urgency, any purpose.

I was twenty-one and I was unreflective and dope-addled, washed along in the hippie current like the spawn of a barnacle. I didn't know anything. I didn't care about anything. I fell in with some people—and their names are on my lips like the taste of sugar, but I won't name them—and these people showed me how to cook heroin and shoot it in my veins, a skinny man like me with no fat to hide those swollen blue conduits to my heart. That lasted two years, weekends mostly, and then a friend OD'd and it scared the holy sweet *literature* out of me. I was no junkie moron, I was a writer, though I didn't actually write anything, but I wasn't hooked on that scene and those people and what we bought for three and five dollars a bag on South Street in Peekskill, where whole blocks were burned out and boarded up in the wake of the Martin Luther King riots. It took me two years more—and the term Quaalude speaks to me here—to get out of there, but get out I did. I wrote a story about those times—"The OD and Hepatitis Railroad or Bust"—and Robley Wilson Jr. published it in *The North American Review*. On the strength of that I applied to Iowa and Iowa accepted me. I'd never been west of New Jersey, and I didn't know Iowa from Ohio—or Idaho, for that matter. But it wasn't all that complicated, really: my girlfriend and my dog climbed into the car, we marked out the route on the map, and headed out on I–80.

It was late summer in Iowa, hills and square-faced buildings and leaves as green as a feat of the imagination. There was a party for new students on a muggy September day in one of those big old houses downtown somewhere, and I remember Fred Exley swaggering in with two shining and beautiful students in tow, one male and one female, and a quart bottle of vodka, from which he was swigging as if it were a big cold translucent beer. It would be many years later, when *Pages From a Cold Island* came out, before I understood where he'd been and what his frame of mind might have been like that day, but at any rate I was impressed: here was a writer. In fact, that first semester I had my choice of studying with one of five writers: Vance Bourjaily, Exley, Gail Godwin, John Irving, or Jack Leggett. I chose Vance, and I chose right. He became my next father/mentor, and the first one I didn't let down. Because I was different now, I was hooked truly and absolutely, and I wasn't going to let anything interfere with getting the words out—or at least wholly giving myself over to the trial for the first time in my life.

Something had happened to me, something inexplicable even to this day: I felt a power in me. I don't mean to get mystical here, because science has killed mysticism for me, to my everlasting regret, but suddenly, though I'd done nothing to earn it, I felt strong, superior, invincible. People said I had a chip on my shoulder—they still do—and I suppose that's right, but what is cockiness, arrogance, whatever you want to call it, but a kind of preemptive strike against your own weaknesses? And without such a strike, what chance is there of succeeding? I felt a power. I wrote. I read everything. I enrolled in the PhD program at the same time I started my MFA, and here I met the last of my academic mentors, Frederick P.W. McDowell, who taught me professionalism and a love of nineteenth-century British literature. (I once made an obscure point about an obscure poet while we were waiting to get into the classroom for his lecture, and he went silent a moment, gave me a wood-stripping look, and said, "Mr. Boyle, I have no doubt that you will ultimately have the discipline to complete the requirements for your doctoral degree, and let me tell you, not all of them do.")

But Vance. Vance was a wonder. He was a rock, calm and collected, and his presence at the other end of the room as he paused to roll a cigarette or make a laconic point was deeply comforting. His was the first class I walked into at the Workshop, and it was all-male. I guess there were maybe fifteen or sixteen students gathered there, most older than I, and all but three (myself included) were writing about their experiences in Vietnam. My story went up the first week. It wasn't about Vietnam. It was about being a hippie in a certain hippie milieu, one who shot dope, and it used a few repeated images to achieve its effect. Vance liked it. My fellow students liked it, with some reservations. It wasn't exactly the kind of experience I'd had in Krishna's class, but I was in a much bigger arena now, and the experience uplifted me (as did Vance's advocacy, later in the semester, of my allegory, "Bloodfall"). In fact, the three writers I was fortunate enough to study with at Iowa—Vance, John Cheever, and Vance's former student, John Irving—were all exceptionally generous and supportive. And that's what a young writer needs to feed his addiction—the kind of praise and gentle criticism that leads to a wider ratification. Yes, you begin to think, I *am* a writer, after all. Not just in the little world I came from, but in the big world, too.

John Cheever was like a wind blowing out of some remote place. He dressed formally, in suits and bow ties, and he spoke with the accent of a time and place none of us had ever been to or even imagined. We must have been equally mystifying to him, with our raggedy hair and beards and clothes the Goodwill would have rejected, but he was game. He didn't have much of an idea of what to do as a teacher, and this was complicated by the fact that he was drunk much of the time, and yet he read our stories carefully and praised them if they were worthy of praise. I kept making noises about "experimental writing" and hailing people like Coover, Pynchon, Barthelme, and John Barth, but Cheever would have none of it. He couldn't make any sense out of *The Sot Weed Factor* and didn't see that it was worth the effort of trying. Further, he insisted that his writing was experimental, too, but I didn't really get what he meant till he published his collected stories five years later and I reread things like "The Death of Justina," as dark and haunting a dream of a story as anything I've read by anyone. All good fiction is experimental, he was telling me, and don't get caught up in fads.

For the next three years most of the writing I did was for my PhD, fifty-page analyses of Tennyson, Keats, and Matthew Arnold and the like, but I'd begun to feel a need for the rush of accomplishment that only fiction could give me and I wrote stories whenever I could. "Descent of Man," "Heart of a Champion," "We Are Norsemen," "The Champ," and "A Women's Restaurant" date from that period, and these stories—mad, absurd, hyperbolic, but mine, all mine—began to appear not only in the smaller magazines, but in *Esquire, The Paris Review,* and *The Atlantic Monthly.* I was a writer. Sure, I was—and there was the proof of it. But when I finished up at Iowa in 1977, I began to realize that there was one more step to take.

Ray Carver had been living in town a few years earlier—in the Cheever days; they drank together at the Mill, and I'll never know why the local historical society hasn't affixed little brass markers to the stools they perched themselves on during those long hard hours of draining glasses and lighting cigarettes, and now he was back to teach in the Workshop. *Will You Please Be Quiet Please?* had come out that year and confirmed what we students had known all along: that Ray was the best short story writer of his time. He amazed and inspired me. We talked about selling stories to little magazines—selling them, that is, once they'd been brought up out of nothing and given shape—but we didn't talk much about craft. In fact, I can't remember discussing craft with anybody then—it was just a given, a path you took because you were a writer able to assimilate all the stories there ever were and make something wholly different out of them and the discomforts and fleeting joys of your own circumscribed life. Anyway, Ray was the apotheosis of what I wanted to become, and I said as much to John Irving once—that is, "I don't want to write novels, only stories, like Ray"—and John opined that I might change my mind someday.

He was right. I did change my mind. With a vengeance. I began *Water Music* on finishing my exams, and spent the next three years on it, all one-hundred-and-four chapters. I began writing in the mornings, seven days a week, the addiction full-blown finally and surely terminal now, and I've been working on that schedule ever since. I had no more idea of how to write a novel when I started *Water Music* than how to write a play when Krishna Vaid asked me to put something up for his workshop ten years earlier. I learned how, though, minute by minute, day by day, and I persisted single-mindedly despite the qualms of both my agent and editor, who couldn't see how the stories of Mungo Park, African explorer, and Ned Rise, pícaro, would ever come together in any kind of even minimally satisfying way. Have faith, I told them, and plowed on, though my editor warned me to bring it in under five-hundred pages (I did, at four-hundred-ninety-six, but I cheated by typing all the way out to the dead white margin of every page).

Then the other books began to accrue and I started to get attention and to sit for interviews and try to articulate what I was attempting to do in my fiction—or rather, what I'd done. I can see how my books and stories are tied inextricably, how the themes and obsessions—the search for the father, racism, class and community, predetermination versus free will, cultural imperialism, sexual war and sexual truce—keep repeating. I can see this, but only in retrospect. That's the beauty of this addiction—you have to move on, no retirement here, look out ahead, though you can't see where you're going. First you have nothing, and then, astonishingly, after ripping out your brain and your heart and betraying your friends and ex-lovers and dreaming like a zombie over the page till you can't see or hear or smell or taste, you have something. Something new. Something of value. Something to hold up and admire. And then? Well, you've got a jones, haven't you? And you start all over again, with nothing.

DORIS GRUMBACH

A View of Writing Fiction From the Rear Window

Frank Conroy, who now heads the Iowa Writers' Workshop after Jack Leggett's retirement, asked for a piece he wants to use in a book of thoughts on writing by (who else?) writers. It did not take very long to do this, since my opinions on the subject are pretty well set in concrete, like those sayings on monuments to presidents in the capital. This is what I sent him, titling it, "A View of Writing Fiction From the Rear Window."

If I had been asked for my views on the craft of writing when I was twenty, or forty, or even sixty, I would have written lyrically, optimistically, egotistically, self-assuredly: I *knew.* I would have celebrated the joys of the craft: freedom from dull, diurnal tasks, the excitement of satisfactory, completed work, the pleasures of recognition and acceptance in a constantly expanding world of my fellow workers, and moderate recompense.

In my sixties, when I taught Workshop students (the wrong word "taught"), I tried to communicate these prospective pleasures to them instead of limiting my instruction to how-to-do-it directions (inevitably *my* way, of course) about writing fiction. My mistake was not realizing that they were already writers when they arrived in Iowa City: All I had to do was hold their coats while they went at it. But still, I hoped they would sense my enthusiasm for the enterprise of writing and the sustaining company of other writers, for the infinite variety of fictional forms, and the joy of finding out you have put one of them into the right words. Inevitably I learned more from those students than they learned from me.

But now I am eighty. I have been "at it" for sixty-four years, ever since high school. I am no longer able to subscribe to those youthful, exalted views. The technological and literary worlds have changed, and I am changed by them. Now I feel out of those worlds, disconnected and removed from them, detached from the extraordinary speed with which the very act of writing is now accomplished. I am among the unhappy few who continue to write by hand, transcribing the scrabbly results to a PC, which then allows me to edit and revise from the printouts without requiring an expensive typist.

What I come up with at last tends to be terse, tight, and lacking in the expansive logorrhea that the ease of the keyboard and the thesaurus encourages. Still, there are times, as now, still using the pen and pad, when I ramble, look too longingly to the past, rely upon my fallible memory rather than practice my old, certain professorial airs.

I wrote my first story in 1934 and submitted it to a contest held yearly in New York City for public high school students. I used a lead pencil and then copied it out in ink. A pencil gripped tightly was then regarded as an effective instrument. It moved slowly, judiciously, at about the same rate as the brain. At graduation, my parents gave me a portable Royal typewriter, which I used for final drafts. I had it with me in graduate school, and on it I typed a thesis on Geoffrey Chaucer, making four messy copies by the use of carbon paper. In thirty years that small instrument never "went down."

I forget whether I sold it or gave it away. I miss it still.

I entered book publishing in a manner no longer (it would seem) common. I was almost forty-four years old. With an alphabetical list of New York publishers in my pocket (I did not know the names of any editors) I traveled an hour to the city and walked from Grand Central Station to the first name on the list— Doubleday—which happened to be located not far from Forty-second Street. I handed the receptionist my brown-paper-wrapped manuscript and went home. I remember why I didn't mail it; I distrusted the post office. It was my only copy. In those careless, eager years I had lost patience with the mess and trouble of carbon paper.

Two weeks later an editor at that publishing house wrote to tell me they would publish it. Two other editors there, Naomi Burton and Ken McCormick, wrote me short notes of encouragement, and an agent, Phyllis Jackson, wrote to say she would be willing to represent my next novel for which Doubleday had offered an option.

During the interval until publication (a period of five months) I met none of these persons, although I lived in Westchester County, about fifty miles from the city. There was no publishing party. I was not required to read or appear anywhere. That first novel and the one that followed in the next year were, as John Leonard once said of his fiction, "secretly published." I had not heard of *Publishers Weekly* or *Kirkus,* and no one thought to inform me of their views on my books. One good notice of the first book, by Granville Hicks, did appear in the *Saturday Review* (to which I subscribed), and there was a paragraph about the second one in a San Diego paper, I think. It had been easy to get published; it was very hard to get notice of any sort that I had been published.

Mine was an obscure beginning. I was discouraged and waited a long time before writing another novel. In those fifteen years I wrote articles and reviews for Catholic periodicals, an unremarkable biography (clearly not my métier), and thought constantly about the novel I wanted to write. I was sixty when I got up my courage to do it, sent it to one editor of note who didn't like it, and then to another who did. This was 1978, still a relatively quiet, gentlemanly time for publishing middle-list fiction. One did not need to submit multiple copies to prospective editors, there were no such things as auctions, huge advances did not exist, talk show appearances were unheard-of. There were almost no readings (those self-gratifying activities of the writer) or other, peripheral activities, referred to as "pushing" the book and "promotion," events that rarely have anything whatever to do with the quality or the craft of writing.

Now, as my friend Sybil is wont to say on many occasions, everything is different since it changed. For most persons (there are notable exceptions, of course) to be a good writer of fiction is no longer to be a faithful practitioner of a difficult craft that requires lifelong practice and a never-ending, incorruptible fidelity to a vision. Most writers now spend much of their time in public, being lionized. They relish the role of public performers. They want to be subjects for personality interviews in newspapers, in magazines, on TV, and on the air. They become national, even international travelers to bookstores, libraries, book-and-author luncheons, and dinner parties, stars at three-day "writing" seminars and two-week summer "writers" workshops.

Writers now "appear," they have become celebrities whose faces, idiosyncrasies, and binges are featured in magazines titled *People* and *The Famous*, and so they are easily recognized by persons who would not think of reading their books. I am aware of only three well-known writers in recent times who have achieved notice by refusing to participate in all these dancing-bear activities: J.D. Salinger, Thomas Pynchon, and Cormac McCarthy. Their reclusiveness and singular devotion to their craft has contrasted interestingly (to the public) with the omnipresence in public of most of the others. Publishers' catalogues and advertisements now list the cities to which their writers will travel on their "book tour" (an oxymoron, almost), as though that was an important selling point and not the unique quality of the work. But it is only fair to add that writers today are not merely victims of their publishers' fondness for publicity. They enjoy displaying themselves and relish the fawning and admiration that accompanies their "appearances."

What does this carping by an old, curmudgeonly person say about the state of the art? That the persona of the writer, in the eyes of the public, has taken the place of the work? That promotion and publicity have replaced practice and performance? I think so, and then I think: Perhaps it is as well. When that often-predicted moment comes when motion pictures, television, and the Internet have obliterated the existence of the book, the publicly celebrated writer will still be there, recognized for himself alone. No one will notice that, seated beside the interlocutor and his publicist in front of a microphone or a camera or on a platform, there is no book in his hand.

Only since the twentieth-century advent of the book jacket have photographs of the writer accompanied the book. I know of no first editions of Herman Melville or Nathaniel Hawthorne that were so embellished. Yet we are still reverently engaged in reading their books. On the other hand, our used, secondhand, and medium-rare bookstore contains numerous first editions of books published after 1950 whose authors have toured, broadcast, been televised and endlessly photographed—but for whose books no customer now ever asks. "Pushing" mediocre fiction has a Sisyphean ending.

There is the question of size, the current, inordinate length of novels. Printed in the new, poorly leaded computer-tight way, the entire oeuvre of Jane Austen would occupy less space than a single work by John Grisham. I have always believed that the extent of a novel was determined by the necessities of its characterization, the requirements of its background and setting, and the inevitable demands of plot. Texture (depth, I suppose) was achieved by exercising careful choice and pruning.

But these days, with the arrival of the word processor (even the name of the instrument equates it with a food grinder), it has become easy and in popular favor to write *a lot,* fatly and fast, creating what the public loves, a long book "to live in," as Francois Mauriac described it, a wrap-around book rather than one that succeeds because of its depth. I have enjoyed watching the reprinting of a contemporary novelist like Penelope Fitzgerald who is a past mistress of condensation and the force of few words. Her longest fiction is less than two-hundred pages. But those pages contain full worlds, complete fictional value, and a marvelous variety of themes, settings, and subject matter.

O, you will counter: What about *War and Peace* and *Remembrance of Things Past* and *The Brothers Karamazov* and *Moby-Dick?* True. They are extensive works. But I take these to be the rare exceptions to my dictum: novels whose content, like Picasso's *Guernica,* justifies a huge panorama. Now that I think of it, I could do with somewhat less cetology in *Moby-Dick,* although its presence does, I suppose, add necessary texture to the novel.

The word processor is responsible for another contemporary failing, the predictable loss of the rich resources of the English language. Equipped with a very limited, automatic thesaurus, it is possible that its universal use will produce an impoverished (and repetitious) fictional prose as PC users lazily resort to the short supply of synonyms in their software programs.

Looking back over what I have written, I see that all these complaints about the present state of things for writers, in writing, and in publishing serious fiction are those of a very old person whose views are skewed, characteristically, by a preference for the way it was, by an ill-humored dislike for what is, and as I am about to express, by a pessimistic view of the future.

Near the end of one's life, the loss of everything—health, strength, illusion, hope—has tended to produce a profound pessimism in some of us. When I was young I was a wholehearted subscriber to Emile Coué's dictum that "every day, in every way, I'm getting better and better." In old age the decline in psychic energy produced a literary pessimism as well. So I find myself expecting a downhill progress in the fiction we will see produced, a sad sea-change, a descent into fast, careless, logorrheic prose, which has created, and then catered to, a lowered literary taste easily satisfied by romantic trash, blockbuster adventure, rapid-fire court and cop tales, mysteries, low-level science fiction (the ignoble descendants of *Brave New World* and *1984*), and sex-laden, *au courant* narratives that celebrate the pornographic.

What is to become of the noble craft of the eighteenth, nineteenth, and the first half of the twentieth centuries, the craft practiced by such disparate writers as Sterne, Fielding, Austen, the Brontës, Dickens, Thackerey, Hawthorne, Melville, Twain, Wharton, Kafka, Chekhov, Tolstoy, Henry James, Thomas Mann, Faulkner, Fitzgerald, O'Connor, Hemingway, *und so weiter?* There are a few arguable survivors of the great tradition, Bellow, Roth, Updike, DeLillo, others perhaps, but then …

Which of the mega-bestsellers (Norman Mailer's term) will our great-grandchildren cherish in the next century? Few, I predict, if any. They will date very fast, their misnamed "perfect" bindings will not hold, their paper will fox and decay, and their very rich authors will disappear into literary oblivion along with their works. But for the millions of copies of their work, whole forests in the state in which I live will have been decimated.

New modes of storytelling have superseded the printed word: motion pictures, computer networks, television, tapes. They are all easier for most people to assimilate. The machine has replaced the mind; the picture, preferably in color, has become a satisfactory substitute for the black-and-white word. Good writing, which once required years of thought and preparation, time, patience, introversion, solitude, a rich field of reference (acquired either through education or constant reading), a cultivated ear and memory, perfect pitch for the sound of words, self-knowledge, and talent, may well disappear under the weight of long, heavy, wordy, mass-produced, instant entertainment.

What good writing does not require is public appearances, lavish cocktail book parties, awards, interviews, lectures, readings, signings, and all the peripheral goings-on and hype of conglomerate, big-city publishing. All these are good for the writer's ego, no doubt, and for the publisher's profits, but they have added nothing to the improvement of craft. It would be very good for writers if they were to disappear into the pages of their books, behind the pictureless jackets. It might help the level of the prose if they would stop "appearing" and performing and become the private persons their craft requires them to be. There is a chance that, slowly, the level of excellence would rise and converge into what we have called literature, even art.

But still: I have a curious, unreasonable, almost mystical faith that, in some cabin in the woods, some small room in a large city, there sits a person, indifferent, even deaf, to the seductions of fame and enriching publishing, who spends endless days and nights wrestling with the art of the word and the sentence, searching himself for insights, images, felicitous phrasing, original ideas and metaphors, and hoping for ultimate success, not on Larry King's show but for the perfect transfer to paper of the world that burns in that writer's mind.

We know nothing of the writer's name or address or sex, or age, for that matter. But it may be that writer whose singular and enduring achievement will be in the hands of many twenty-first-century readers.

ETHAN CANIN

Smallness and Invention
or, What I Learned at the Iowa Writers' Workshop

I came to the Iowa Writers' Workshop in August of 1982, having driven across the country in a '67 Mustang hardtop that was gradually becoming a convertible. The stitching was coming out in the roof upholstery, and huge panels of it hung down inside the car like shades, which I pinned up again with safety pins so that I could see out the windows. I was twenty-two years old. I had bought the Mustang with money I had received that year from *Redbook* magazine for a story I had written in a writing class at Stanford University, where until June I had been an undergraduate. I was too young to be coming to Iowa.

I didn't know it at the time. At the time it seemed like an adventure, not just to be moving to an unheard-of place a thousand miles from any ocean—people laughed when I told them: They said, "Io-wa?"—but to be pursuing what had come to me in a late-night romantic reverie as my true calling. I had started out college as a mechanical engineering major, had taken physics and math classes for my first two years before idly stumbling one day onto the collected stories of John Cheever, a thick red paperback book that changed my life. Perhaps it was the normal maturation of a brain, but suddenly as a sophomore in college I decided that the

fixity of engineering, the precision and derivability that had so
drawn me as an eighteen-year-old, was now limiting. I wanted a
field in which nobody, not even the experts, knew anything. This
field, I understood, was writing.

Well, perhaps it was not writing but literature. That year in a
required lecture course I had read Dostoyevsky's *Notes From
Underground*, Freud's *Civilization and Its Discontents*, and Gide's
The Immoralist, books I would never in ten lifetimes have read on
my own. Yet all of them had captured me with the power of
their assertions—assertions that, most fascinating of all, seemed
unprovable. Here were dark claims about the human soul, put
forward with no basis at all except hunch, and here was I,
trained in the rigor of mathematical proof and logical progression, absolutely seized with the truth—or at least the possibility
of truth—of what was before me. Flipping through the
Engineering section of the course catalog one day I wandered
forward a single page to English. There I found a course: creative
writing.

A few weeks later I sat down on my first day and watched our
instructor, who rumor had it was a *published* writer, twist rubber
bands over his hands until his knuckles turned white. The students around me were a different sort—many looked sad, somehow dissipated in their features, uniformly poorly dressed, the
way I hadn't seen anyone look in my engineering courses. I had
been reading the Cheever stories every night before sleep, and in
my narrow dormitory bed had exalted in his prose.

Her smile, her naked shoulder had begun to trouble the
indecipherable shapes and symbols that are the touch-
stones of desire, and the light from the lamp seemed to
brighten and give off heat and shed that unaccountable
complacency, that benevolence, that the spring sunlight
brings to all kinds of fatigue and despair. Desire for her
delighted and confused him. Here it was, here it all was,

and the shine of the gold seemed to him then to be all around her arms.

"The Pot of Gold," from The Stories of John Cheever

Here it was for me, too, here it all was—reading until early morning while across the room my roommate snored his plain old snores. I felt every night that in my hands was the key to another world.

How could I justify such softness? An engineer, a student who had always disdained the lack of rigor outside the sciences? In my creative writing class I decided that I would write like John Cheever, that I would seek those elongated phrases, those elided leaps into the world of ardor and transcendence and unearthed human longing that shone in his stories like gems beneath a stream. Here was the chance to unbridle myself of the rigor I had loved and, only now, I realized, had also always wanted to shed. How far superior this raw emotion seemed to me. How much more profound and complex a truth. Exultant from my reading, I sat down and wrote a story.

It was dismal. My teacher grimaced when he handed it back to me. It contained elements of Cheever, elements of James Joyce's "Araby," which I had read that year as well, and elements of Gide—a maudlin poem in prose celebrating the unlocked door to the human spirit. My teacher wrote, "Perhaps you should give us a few details."

Perhaps, indeed. I was wounded, but went back to Cheever. There again I found rejuvenation, found his unbridled emotion electrifying:

... It seemed then to be a sense of pride, an aureole of lightness and valor, a kind of crown. He seemed to hold the crown up to scrutiny and what did he find? Was it merely some ancient fear of Daddy's razor strap and Mummy's scowl, some childish subservience to the bullying world? He well knew his instincts to be rowdy, abundant, and indiscreet and had he allowed the world and all its tongues to impose upon him some structure of transparent values for the convenience of a conservative economy, an established church, and a bellicose army and navy? He seemed to hold the crown, hold it up into the light, it seemed made of light and what it seemed to mean was the genuine and tonic taste of exaltation and grief.

"The World of Apples," from The Stories of John Cheever

With that emotion coursing through me again, I sat down and wrote another story. Again dismal. It was pure emotion, I see now when I look at it, a story at a fever pitch from the opening words. Handing it back, my teacher grimaced again.

So I went back one more time to Cheever. This time I looked more closely at *how* he wrote. Perhaps such a reflex for analysis was a remnant of what I had learned in my engineering classes, that even the most complex motion could be understood when broken into its component vectors. I began typing out some of Cheever's great paragraphs. I simply sat down and typed:

... Alice strode to the door, opened it, and went out. A woman came in, a stranger looking for the toilet. Laura lighted a cigarette and waited in the bedroom for about ten minutes before she went back to the party. The Holinsheds had gone. She got a drink and sat down and tried to talk, but she couldn't keep her mind on what she was saying.

The hunt, the search for money that had seemed to her natural, amiable, and fair when they first committed themselves to it, now seemed like a hazardous and piratical voyage. She had thought, earlier in the evening, of the missing. She thought now of the missing again. Adversity and failure accounted for more than half of them, as if beneath the amenities in the pretty room a keen race were in progress, in which the loser's forfeits were extreme. Laura felt cold. She picked the ice out of her drink with her fingers and put it in a flower vase, but the whiskey didn't warm her. She asked Ralph to take her home.

"The Pot of Gold," from The Stories of John Cheever

In my own development as a writer, I suppose this was as important an exercise as I have ever performed.

I discovered two things: first, that Cheever's great, epiphanic leaps were almost invariably preceded (and followed, it turned out) by paragraphs that accumulated small, accurate detail. Initially, this seemed like a profoundly important discovery to me. I could absolutely engage the fever pitch of emotion that had seduced me into writing in the first place, so long as I balanced it with large amounts of pedestrian observation. I went back to the stories I had written and added detail, surrounded my epiphanies with line after line of small-scale particulars.

But this alone did not make what I'd written much better, and it was here that I made my second, although admittedly in Cheever's case, unproved discovery: that the progression from detail to epiphany is not a technique used merely for its effect on the reader, but that this method is in fact how a writer discovers his own material.

This changed my writing forever. To put it another way: I had chanced upon the discovery that for the writer it is not moral pondering or grand emotion that are the entrance to a story, but detail and small event. The next story I wrote I started not with the feeling of grandeur that had been my inspiration before, but with a narrowed concentration. I began by imagining a single act: a man going for a swim in San Francisco Bay. I didn't start with any message in mind; I didn't start with any climactic emotions swirling around me; I just started with the swim. What I discovered was that as I wrote these details, as I imagined myself striding down to the dirty shore, as I imagined myself plunging into the chilly water, stroking against the hard current, the story itself came to me. And it was not the story I intended. It seemed to be a story that came not from me but from this character, a salty old guy who swam in cold water. The amazing thing was, by the end, I had actually pitched myself up to the same feverish swirl that had been my old inspiration. The difference was that this time the fever was the result of the story and not the cause. I remember that the story was actually easy to write (perhaps the last one, alas, that I will ever know). And *Redbook* published it. And I bought myself the Mustang.

After that, I came to Iowa.

I stopped writing. Almost immediately and almost completely. Why? I think it was because suddenly, now, added to the normal difficulty of invention was the stultifying pressure of observation. Everything I wrote was going to be looked at. For a year and a half I wrote nothing. What a secret I kept, walking around this idyllic Midwestern town, going to readings, talking about literature, meeting with my peers to read their new stories and handing them my old ones, pieces that I'd written in college. I was too young at the time to realize what a gift those two years in Iowa City were, how extravagant I was to waste them, and too young also to feel the unbearable guilt that an older person would have felt at such a wasted opportunity.

But not only do we learn in unpredictable ways, we also learn unpredictable things. I didn't realize then that what I would take away from Iowa was the rudiments of one of the most important skills a writer can learn, a skill that has nothing to do with prose style or pacing or narrative structure, and everything to do with inspiration. A writer's lifelong battle, I learned that year (although I didn't know I had learned it till later), is the battle to sustain the imagination, to discover the tricks of habit that allow invention to proceed in the face of conformity. As it turns out, I had to write thirty pages or so just to reach the required length for my thesis. By now, I had come to the end of my final year, and the pressure I felt as I sat down to write was overpowering. Not only did I need to write two stories (and fast), but I needed to write two *great* stories. That was actually how I felt sitting down to begin. I only realize now that this feeling was a close cousin to the old feeling I used to have, the old frenzy of emotion that had been my initial inspiration to write.

Nothing, of course, came of my attempts. I sat frozen at the keys for hours at a time, imagining not only completed stories, but stories already on their swift flight to acclaim. I saw readers moved, as I was, to inexplicable tears. In this manner I wrote four, five, six beginnings. Then I gave up.

As it turns out, the only thing that saved me was the despondency that finally forced me to abandon grandiosity and start once again with small event. A week or two later I sat down, deflated, nearly panicked, and simply tried to write the beginning of a minor episode. I had no idea where the episode would go, but I started by imagining a man whose neighbor wants to cut down his elm tree. Nothing more. No hopes. No messages. No finale.

The only way to circumvent the pressure was to sneak in around it, I discovered, to trick the mind, which so easily runs ecstatically or dismally ahead of itself, onto a path of small invention. That path, it seems to me, is a maze, and the writer is not above it but inside it.

Starting small, I wrote two stories. And I wrote them in a couple of weeks. I had no idea whether they "worked," as my fellow students might say, but I felt at least that the events in them led one to the next. I felt that way because that was how I had written them, as a follower and not as a leader. I had learned, I now see, to enter the realm of imagination through the hidden door of small event and let the story show itself to me. This was an invaluable lesson, though I had no idea I had learned it at the time. The stories were good enough for my degree, at least, and in May of 1984 I received it, a nearly worthless sheet of black and gold, like earth against corn.

That summer I left Iowa finally and headed west again in the Mustang, windows open to what was now the powerfully nostalgic smell of a Midwestern evening. Just as I hit cruising speed on Highway 80, the roof upholstery popped loose again, flapping down across my vision, and I reached over and tacked it up again with the old safety pins. Then I closed the window, pressed the accelerator to the floor, and zoomed down the incline toward Nebraska, headed toward California and the rest of my life. Little had changed, I thought. I had learned nothing in two years. I was deeply discouraged; but in my hidden heart I was also relieved, I think, to know that I did not have inside me what it would take to become a writer, relieved to know that I would not have to follow this most difficult life that I knew then that writing was.

STUART DYBEK

Ralston

I remember the year, the morning, the very moment that my life as a writer began. I remember exactly what I wrote, the phrase that transformed words into a thrill—a discovery that set the act of writing free from the cell of a school subject called English. English was spelling tests, diagramming, tedious exercises in workbooks, but writing became a jailbreak of the imagination. What I don't remember, and so still don't understand, is why in that same year I went from a student with straight A's in Catechism and no check marks in Conduct—a kid who just the grade before had been told by the nun that he might have a chance to become the first St. Stuart— to a bad boy.

It was a winter morning in fourth grade. I'd been awakened during the night by the sound of my mother retching in the bathroom, and so wasn't surprised when she didn't get me up for school. Instead, my father, who should have already been at work at the Harvester plant where he was a foreman, shook me awake a good hour earlier than necessary.

"Rise and shine, sonny boy," he said. "Ma's got the flu. You've got to get yourself off to school. The snow's coming down out there, so wear your earmuffs and galoshes. I made your breakfast. It's on the table." Then, he rushed off, late.

My winter routine was to drape my underwear for the next day on the radiator each night before going to bed. In the morning, I'd reach for the warm underwear and then strip my flannel pajamas off under the feathertick *piersyna* in which my grandmother had once swaddled her firstborn son, my father, when they'd come across from Poland. But this morning I noticed that my underwear was barely warm. I guessed that, with my mother sick, my father hadn't had a chance to stoke the furnace at his regular hour.

A year earlier, my father had bought the six-flat apartment building to which we'd moved. The steam heat for each apartment was generated by a coal furnace in the basement. Now that he was a landlord, my father would rise at five A.M. on winter mornings to stoke the furnace before leaving for work. If he didn't, Mrs. Boudena, the tenant right above us, would bang on her radiator, a sound like convicts raking their tin cups on the prison bars.

But she was quiet today, perhaps in deference to the snow-muffled grind of traffic on Twenty-fifth Street. And minus the company of the radio my mother always played, broadcasting news, weather, and Frank Sinatra, our apartment was not only chillier but quieter than usual, too. The light seemed faint and frosted as it filtered through screens clotted with snow. One of my father's many planned projects was storm windows, but we couldn't afford them yet. I sat down at the kitchen table before the breakfast he'd made for me: a bowl of Hot Ralston and a mug of chocolate-flavored Ovaltine.

On good days breakfast might be French toast with Log Cabin syrup poured from the chimney spout of a tin can shaped like a log cabin, and washed down with the hot chocolate my mother beat from scratch into a foam dusted with cinnamon and topped with marshmallow fluff. Or eggs, soft-boiled if my mother made them, served with toast and a strip of bacon, or, as my father made them on Sunday mornings, scrambled with sliced kielbasa. Usually though, breakfast was cereal, which was perfectly fine until the weather turned cold. Then the Rice Krispies, Puffed Wheat, Kix, Cheerios, and Wheaties would be put away like summer clothes, to be replaced by hot, stick-to-the-ribs cereals: oatmeal, okay if camouflaged by raisins and honey, or Cream of Wheat, which even the dissolving nuggets of brown sugar barely made palatable. Worse by far was Hot Ralston.

Hot Ralston was, obviously, supposed to be served hot, but the gob in the bowl before me had grown cold. It looked alien and foreboding like a lunar landscape. At least I was spared from inhaling the steam with its mashy, woolly smell that forecast a texture of sandpaper mixed with wallpaper paste. The name itself—Ralston—sounded scratchy, tweed on the tongue. A friend at school named Benny Kotteck, whom everyone, naturally, called Kotex, said that he'd once had a nightmare in which after having his tonsils removed, instead of ice cream or Jell-O, they'd brought him Ralston.

The sorry fact was that I'd brought both Ovaltine and Ralston upon myself. Ovaltine was my first fiasco. It took twenty-five cents and the seal from a jar of Ovaltine to acquire a Captain Midnight code ring that allowed me to decipher the messages in secret code broadcast to the Midnight Rangers at the end of each episode. I'd also splurged for an Ovaltine shaker—it resembled a martini shaker painted white and red—in which the Ovaltine was shaken with ice and then poured out frothy cold like a chocolate malt. When I took my first long thirsty slug, I was shocked. It didn't taste like chocolate, or any other flavor for that matter, although there was something vaguely familiar about its awful aftertaste. I braved another sip and identified it: a malt of grainy dried dog chow, ice, and milk.

So, when I mounted my campaign for Ralston, my parents agreed to buy it only after adding the stipulation that I damn well better eat it. Ralston sponsored the Tom Mix cowboy show that I listened to on the radio—we didn't have a television yet. There was a jingle that went:

> *Ask your mother in the morning*
> *To serve you up a steaming plate.*
> *It's a grand, hot, whole-wheat cereal,*
> *And the cowboys think it's great.*

There was a Ralston Straight Shooter Pledge: *I promise to shoot straight with Tom Mix by regularly eating good old Hot Ralston, the official Straight Shooter's cereal, because I know Hot Ralston is just the kind of cereal that will help build a stronger America.*

For a box top and a quarter you could get an issue of *Tom Mix Commando Comics.* I got the one in which Tom and the cowboys were fighting a squadron of real flying dragons from Japan.

My mother made my breakfasts, and I'd struck a deal with her that I'd only be served Ralston and Ovaltine once a week and never in combination. At that rate, it seemed I'd be in high school before I'd finished them. But despite my Straight Shooter pledges, my father knew my welsher tendencies and he'd instinctively dished up the dreaded Ralston/Ovaltine one-two. He'd lived through the Depression and was determined that I would belong to the Clean the Plate Club.

I filled a soup bowl with Ovaltine and set it on the floor for our cat Whiskers. A sniff was enough to drive Whiskers from the room, so I carried it into the bathroom and flushed it down the toilet.

I prodded the Ralston with my spoon. If anything, cold Hot Ralston seemed even pastier than hot Hot Ralston. I experimented, flicking a few balls of it from my finger onto the walls where it stuck. An idea came to me. Admittedly it was inspired by my buddy Angel Rivera, who'd recently constructed a snowball with a dogshit center—an invention that got him and his desk banished to the corridor outside our classroom—the vantage point from which Angel and I observed much of fourth grade. I formed the Ralston into a ball, about the size of a cue ball—my father believed in generous portions—and then opened the door to the backyard and rolled the ball in the deep snow at either side of the print from my father's overshoes on the top stair. The snow was good packing and made a beautiful projectile: a white snowball concealing a core of leaden, disgusting-looking Ralston. For all anyone who was hit in the face with it would know, it might be a ball of boogers—an incredibly potent weapon in the snowball fights that spontaneously erupted on the way to school. I set it in the freezer to put a little crust on it.

With breakfast quickly disposed of, there was time to kill before having to leave for school, especially since my father had awakened me earlier than usual. Time enough for the homework that once again I hadn't done to nag at me. Lately, missed homework nagged at me every night before I fell asleep, and I'd wake guilty each morning, not that such feelings had caused me to reform. I don't know why I stopped doing my homework in fourth grade; I'd done it faithfully before.

Our teacher was Sister Mary Relenete. There was a businesslike coldness about her, a sharpness of manner accentuated by her physical appearance: ice blue eyes, a pointy slant to her nose upon which balanced the frameless little glasses she wore, pale lips set too tight to either smile or frown. She was thin, but hardly frail, thin in a way that looked severe and threatening, a thinness empowered by the restrained rage of self-denial.

I couldn't have articulated any of that, but I felt it; I think we all did, as Sister Relenete's reputation for not tolerating what she called "monkey shines" proceeded her. Her policy on homework was cut and dry: If you didn't do it, punishment was swift.

Those of us who didn't had formed a secret society called Club Slappa. It was boys only. Kotex was a charter member, as was Waxman—Sherman Waxmonski—an up-and-coming psychopath. There was my best buddy, Angel Rivera, and Juan Augusto, whom everyone called Wanny rather than Juanito. Membership varied depending on the assignment, but on any given day there'd be maybe a half dozen of us.

We'd find out who early on, right after prayer and saluting the flag, when Sister Relenete would ask, "Hands from who doesn't have his homework."

Slowly, our rising hands would betray us.

She'd express her disapproval—a *th-th* sucked through her teeth—and then, "Up front!" she'd command in her characteristically succinct way. "March!"

Heads bowed, we'd begin our silent march down the corridor to the nurse's office. I'd never seen a nurse in that office, but sometimes when kids got sick in class they'd be made to wait there until their parents came for them. Sister Relenete would enter first, and at her signal, one at a time we'd follow her in.

Standing outside in the corridor, awaiting our turn, we'd listen for the sharp report of Sister Relenete's bony hands striking flesh. In her class, the first missed assignment was met with a stern warning; the second resulted in having to stand outside the nurse's office, listening to the others being punished without being called in yourself; from the third time on—"three strikes and you're out," she'd say—missing homework got you one business-like slap in the face.

Initially, it seemed a tolerable trade-off. But now, for the unrepentant hard core she was dealing out two slaps, a solid right and a particularly stinging left in combination. They had a consistent, discernible rhythm: a single sucking of her teeth preceded the first staccato *whap!*; then, after a double suck, the more resounding left—*whappa!*

"Like Lawrence Welk," Waxman observed, "a-one-and-a-two." *Th-whap-th-th-whappa.* Club Slappa.

We'd march back into class, the emblems of our fraternity of laziness and pain emblazoned on our cheeks in flaming finger marks. The stylish way for reentering the classroom was with a cocky grin, especially as those who weren't regulars would sometimes return fighting back tears. Waxman had become quite cavalier about it, affecting boredom, not even bothering to smile. He told us that he'd practice at night, getting his face in shape by whapping himself, and that before he went to sleep he'd apply a rinse from a dill pickle jar to his cheeks, a secret he'd learned from an uncle who boxed in the Marines and used brine to toughen his knuckles.

Nonchalance eluded me. The wait in the corridor played on my nerves. It was similar to waiting for the dentist or to get a tetanus shot. I didn't like the way the heat of her handprint numbed my face into a twitchy countenance that was barely under my control. I never knew what expression I was marching back into class with, or if the quivering I felt through my body would become a quaver shuddering aloud from the back of my throat.

Earlier in the week, after dealing out two slaps each, Sister Relenete had remarked, "Since this doesn't seem to be getting home to you boys, the next time we might have to introduce you to the Irish Burn."

I wasn't sure of what the Irish Burn was, but it sounded ominous. Waxman said it was having your sideburns tweaked—he actually used the word *tweaked*. "A weird pain like you never felt before," he chuckled in his demented way; then his hand darted out in demonstration. I ducked, but for the fraction of a second that he'd managed to tweak a sideburn the pain was indeed both novel and excruciating.

The homework I hadn't done was for Geography, a subject I liked. We were studying Africa, the Dark Continent, where the Church had missions through which one could "buy" a Pagan baby, not that the baby would actually be delivered to Chicago, but it would be baptized in your name—providing it was a Christian name. That left me out: Until I elevated the name to sainthood there wouldn't be any Stuarts running around Africa. Sister Relenete had assigned a composition on Africa that was to be one page of loose-leaf paper long.

I cleared a space on the breakfast table where the bowl of Ralston had sat and in blue ballpoint pen began to write as large as I could in hopes of filling the page. Instead of writing about the missions, I began by listing animals; it was the animals that most interested me about Africa. I listed a few tribes that I'd heard about, as well (badly misspelling *pygmies* I'd learn when my graded paper was returned to me). I wrote about the cries of birds and roars of lions, about packs of hyenas, herds of zebra, about monkeys and gorillas, all animals I'd seen at the Brookfield Zoo. Now, at the breakfast table, I was seeing them in their natural habitat. By the light of snow, I wrote about the heat and flies and the jungle. When I tried to describe how tall the trees were I was stuck for a moment, mute with awe. Grasping for a comparison, I thought of the tallest things I'd ever seen, which were the skyscrapers downtown, and I wrote the phrase *the tree-scraped skies*.

It was as if a bolt shot through me—the spark that leaps between opposite poles in the laboratories of mad doctors intent on creating life. And why not? After all, I had just invented metaphor.

I quickly finished the composition—it finished itself—but I kept returning to that phrase: *the tree-scraped skies*. Each time I read it, I'd get a charge of excitement that I'd never felt before from homework.

I needed to show someone. For the first time in my life I wanted to read my work aloud. I raced down the hallway to the front of the house, to my parent's bedroom where my mother lay half-asleep, spent and pale, looking bleached out in the frosted light. There was a bucket half-filled with water beside her bed in case a wave of nausea should overcome her and she couldn't make it to the bathroom.

"Sweetheart, you should be off to school," she mumbled.

"Want to hear my composition for Geography?"

Not waiting for her reply, I began to read, building up to *the tree-scraped skies*, but before I could utter those words aloud, a wave of nausea overcame her and she leaned gagging and retching over the side of the bed, her groans amplified by the metal bucket. It wasn't the response I'd been hoping for.

If this were fiction it would be called "Africa." I'd title it that in deference to the Africa of the imagination, for it was imagination that illuminated my childhood, imagination that saved me. Saved me from what, I can't tell in abridgment, but saved me nonetheless. It wasn't necessary at the time to recognize the power of imagination in order to employ it. Instinctively, imagination became the ultimate defense; it wasn't, as some would have it, a dreamer's way of escaping from reality, but rather an active power by which through language one reshaped the world, overlaying images of alternative possibility and the beauty of change over static images of defeat. And because its vision implied change, it was a subversive power—one that instinctively requires a fiction writer's first allegiance.

But this isn't fiction. No departures were necessary. All I've had to do was to describe what happened that morning when with a few words I made an image that I could never have drawn with charcoal or paint. I've remembered it like this for a long time, though I can't recall just when it was that I became conscious of remembering it in a way that turned the image of Africa into the story of Ralston and transformed the simple, visual image of *tree-scraped skies* into the more complicated, active image of a boy sitting at the breakfast table beside an empty cereal bowl on a snowy morning, composing a line that changed his life.

I remember other such moments that have to do with writing with the same sure sense of recall, clearly etched, the way one recalls early sexual encounters—a first kiss, a first feel, a first crush: the composition in sixth grade when we were told to write a Christmas story from the point of view of one of the characters in the stable at Bethlehem, and I wrote a story called "The Enormous Gift," told by an ant who brought the baby Jesus a crumb of bread that weighed a hundred times the weight of my narrator. Our teacher, Sister Edmond, did read that story aloud, just as later, in high school, my freshman English teacher, Mr. Hedlund, who doubled as the school janitor, read aloud the story I wrote in response to a How I Spent My Summer assignment. It was a story about a fishing trip a gang of us called the Fuckups (I left that out of my essay) had taken, riding our bikes down the railroad tracks to where the black hoboes fished from a trestle above the Chicago Sanitary Canal, known in the neighborhood as Shit Creek. Our gear was nylon fishing line wound around clothespins; we disguised our hooks with dough bait balls of Wonder Bread. Clambering on the girders, my buddy Jerry Stambula, as gifted an athlete as I've ever seen, fell in. He never did as well in sports after that dunking, and by senior year the only sport he went out for was the bowling team. I caught a strange, sickly white, eyeless fish with deformed fins and cancers erupting from its body like yellow parasites. None of us would touch it. Dusk was coming on, turning the rusty black bridge bronze. We left the fish hooked, dangling on fishing line from the bridge. Angel gave the line a tug to set it in metronomic motion, *swinging the fish*, I wrote in my composition, *like an altar boy swings a censer*.

That image was in itself a fiction, not exactly how it happened at the time, but I saw it that way when I wrote it. I remembered when Angel was an altar boy, before he was expelled from Catholic school, and thought maybe it was funny to compare a stinking fish with an incense-fuming censer. In my imagination, the fish like the bridge had turned bronze with dusk.

After I'd read my composition aloud, Mr. Hedlund—English teacher by day, school janitor by night—turned my moment of acclaim into humiliation by asking, "Dybek, do you ever write poetry?"

By senior year in high school, I'd read some poets on my own, the Beats—Kerouac, Ginsburg, Corso—and returned to the setting of the Sanitary Canal for the first piece I ever wrote that wasn't an assignment. It was a prose-poemish story written to entertain my friends, who all read each month's *Mad Magazine* as if it were a samizdat. Titled "Opus Turd," my story was told from the point of view of a turd floating down the canal. It began "Waste and juice and I am born …"

It ended with the final cry of my rapidly dissolving narrator: "I must see it all! I must see it all!"

The images are still imprinted on my memory, and within each image a story is compressed, at ready to be told. Image by image, or should I say thrill by thrill, I can recall each fledgling attempt to remake the world out of language. What seemed random at the time—events easily lost in the mindless chaos called education—has now been sorted out and arranged by hindsight into a narrative progression: the spine of a writing life, while all the tests and make-work assignments have receded to a gray blur of words and numbers that never added up to a single vision, let alone to an aspect of identity.

Yet, given that recall, I remain puzzled as to why I can still summon up a writing assignment in fourth grade so clearly, but don't remember why my behavior radically changed that year, never to change back again through the rest of my time in school. Was there some connection between the thrill, the emergence of a secret self of the imagination, imagination with its subversive allure, and becoming a class clown?

That day I wrote the composition on Africa and in the process accidentally discovered metaphorical thinking, I returned from school to find my mother feeling better, though not yet well enough to cook dinner. My father came home from work with a fresh loaf of Gonella Italian bread, and after doing his chores as a landlord—we shoveled the sidewalks around the house together and then he tended the furnace—he cleaned the kitchen and began cooking his specialty, spaghetti and meatballs, one of my favorites. We ate supper later than usual. He'd set the table with soup bowls, which is the way he said Italians ate spaghetti. In my bowl, instead of a meatball, there rested the melting snowball of Ralston that my father had found in the freezer. In my excitement, I'd forgotten to take it to school.

"Eat, sonny boy," he smiled, and seasoned it for me with a little snowfall from the foil green container of Kraft's Parmesan cheese.

JAYNE ANNE PHILLIPS

The Widow Speaks

Kenneth Tynan's widow Kathleen, in her introduction to his letters, states, first line, "Writers hate to write, almost all of them." She goes on to describe, in loving remembrance, her husband "blocked in the main endeavor of a book or an article" turning to his journal, "where he might deliver himself of a self-punishing complaint about his own indolent and hateful character." Writers do chastise themselves, with seriousness and skill, as though it were a matter of personal failure not to be steadily equal to one's talent—to the talent one has displayed formerly, or even concurrently with the present hiatus. Some turn with relief to letter writing or diaries, free of the pressure of perfection, choosing words to entertain or communicate. Happy at the prospect of a wholeheartedly interested listener, the writer engages a distant correspondent or some version of a private, non-artist self—the smaller self who stands always at the threshold of writing, like a person in a doorway who knows better than to enter the room. Others write their own work or nothing at all. They remain silent and use the pressure in their own way. Allowing themselves no comforts, they "reserve the right not to write." Putting pen to paper, fingers to keyboard, is always a risk, as the writer well knows.

We might compare getting started on a story to starting a relationship (oh, that first time together, lying down skin-to-skin!), or beginning a novel to committing to a marriage. Each long-term liaison is laden with its own miracles and traps: There is the young marriage, the first marriage, the late marriage in which indolent time does not exist and all is revealed at the first touch. There is the ecstasy-inducing, doomed, bipolar heights-and-depths marriage, and the brain-shattering cataclysm that never achieves consummation but is instead an extended hallucinatory preparation. There is the deep, long, enduring marathon that wakes and sleeps, steadily increasing as pages mount and the light shifts day to night, season to season. All are relationships that stay alive until the book is done and moves beyond the mind that lived within it. The love affair, like a years-long phase of sexual intoxication between lovers, is over, and the book takes with it a newly created soul bound to no human being, no physical time or sensory need. It is alive and it may live for hundreds of years, unsullied, undiminished. It may be read or lie dormant but remains supremely itself, tension strung, pitch and nuance perfectly attune, a world preserved in love and grief, continually reborn.

To what, then, do we compare not writing, not finishing the story, putting the novel aside in anguish? Admit it or not, we compare these to death, the little death or the big death, sexual connotations intended, and we think of *not writing* (in the pause between projects, in the stalled eye of a novel) as death itself. Nothing more horrible, no failure of nerve more acute, than to be a writer and not write, to never write, perhaps, to stop, *to decide to stop,* not to hope for writing or want it, to let go of writing, to swear it off like drugs or sex with the wrong party, or some other terrible compulsion that will finally tear one apart—decimating the room and maiming anyone in the house. The writer not writing is a wholly guilty party, like someone who through anger or terrible neglect has killed off his own life's mate, counterpart, reason to live. Or the writer not writing is completely disengaged, a ghostly anar-

chist traversing Rimbaud's desert mountains and plateaus, a purveyor of mule team commerce seldom in reach of a human voice
and never the accents of home, a gun-running, slave-trading mentor to wild boys, for the fire that consumes itself leaves more than
ashes. A mesmerizing remnant haunts the barren sand and stone
streets of Abyssinian Harar, an unrelenting centrifugal force that
pulls into itself those drawn to conflagration, to total surrender, as
though we might know—in an instant of silence—all Rimbaud
made himself forget, all he denied when he turned his back on
writing and lived beyond it, in exile.

Silence is the writer's familiar. Silence, earned or merely present, is as natural to writers as writing. It fills the space between
words, behind words. Silence, amniotic and replete, is the auditory
equivalent of the empty page. Images and pictures float within it.
The work of entering them remains organic and mysterious, like
anything we don't understand in thoughts, in words *about*.
Personality or intellect can bite the hands that feed it, so to speak.
The writer, inside or outside a book, may find himself in a sus-
pended horror of confusion with everything at stake. The work of
a skilled technician does not break through; work that lasts must
glimpse the miraculous and exist apart, defining its own truth. "At
last," Frank Conroy told his first fiction workshop, "you hold the
story in your hands. It's all there: the faultless curve of head and
limb, the opalescent eyelids, the perfect little fingernails. Now you
ask yourself, is it a dead baby or a live baby?"

A writer stays alive because he or she is writing, or may write: the
elusive divine exists. "No such thing as a bad day," a poet friend grum-
bled sardonically, "more like a bad decade." "It may be my fourth
novel," said another writer, "but this one doesn't know I wrote the
other three." "That novel in you has to come out," says doctor to
patient in a particularly mordant *New Yorker* cartoon. "Writing is like
heroin," said a writer acquainted with both, "but writing is peak
engagement—like mainlining consciousness. There's this extended
wham that you have to sustain by living with your veins open."

"Writing?" comments another. "It's basic to certain monstrosities." "I'm selfish enough," said the despairing mother of four children and two novels, "but I can't *think*. If I could think, I could write." Told she'll write later, she responds, "Later, it won't be me. I won't be here later." Asked about balancing writing/politics/maternity, Grace Paley told a group of young women in Iowa City, "Don't have a little, narrow life. Have a big life." "I can't stand hearing writers moan about writing," sniffs a rather successful practitioner of humorous novels, "and I would *never* spend more than two years on a book." "Face it," says an award-winning essayist, "we don't write for readers. Why should we? Most readers figure a book is a book if it's between covers, and they'd rather watch television anyway." "We write for the self we ought to measure up to, the Zen thread in the muslin shroud," says the Buddhist poet. "James Agee was right," says the novelist known for her evocations of place. "We write for the part of us that knows where we're going, but on pain of death would never tell us." "See you further along the trail," Ray Carver told a compatriot writer at a conference. "You make money doing readings?" queried a fiction writer's older brother. "You mean people pay you to read things you've already written?" "I suppose they really should pay more if I made it up on the spot," she told him, "but it doesn't work that way." "Amazing," confides one writer to another, after each was introduced as the other at a literacy benefit auction, "they always find a way to humiliate you." "But—it's *you*," a friend says to a writer describing an excruciating block. "How can you not control *yourself*?"

The question may seem aberrant, something a dimwit or sadistic mother might ask her charge during toilet training, but Americans do regard living writers as both needlessly and necessarily strange. They tend to regard dead writers as history. And history, other than the Spielburg/Stone cinematic variety, is particularly anathema in our current incarnation. History, *he's history*, equates with non-relevance. For those on the North American isle of relative safety, history is yesterday or last week; the big picture is never in focus. Americans don't do politics, though we live in a barrage of tabloid reductions of ideas and events. Writers do politics. Any story is a history in which politics and event are portrayed in human terms—not as tract, but as inquiry, warning, requiem.

How instructional to remember that the crises of history, the political firestorms of our own and other brutal centuries, have stopped writers only by killing them. In those times, imprisoned, diseased, mourning, the writer, as long as she can think and wonder, writes. Her family and country destroyed, Marina Tsvetayeva wrote. Following the shifting allegiances of her husband from post-Revolution exile in Prague and Paris back to wartime Russia, famine and doom, she wrote. As the Germans advanced on Moscow, her fifteen-year-old son wanted to put on a uniform and fight. Concerned for his safety, she left penurious employment as a translator and moved them to rural Siberia in an attempt to join evacuated writers more acceptable to the State. Ostracized, she was allowed no work permit and no work, even in the kitchens. A policeman in the village who allowed her to do his laundry was reprimanded. Finally, one daughter dead, her husband and surviving daughter imprisoned, excoriated for her part in their troubles by the son she adored, Tsvetayeva (who had written in her journal, "I do not want to die. I want not to be," and then "Rubbish ... so long as I am needed") hung herself. Her son, whose fortunes she thought may have eased with her death, did not attend her funeral and enlisted immediately. A few months later, he died defending Moscow.

No longer needed! Jerzy Ficowski, in his introduction to Bruno Schultz' *The Street of Crocodiles*, refers to "the profaned time of everyday life, which relentlessly subordinates all things to itself and carries events and people off in a current of evanescence." Schultz' material was the transformed history of his childhood and native town. Talented artist, reclusive secondary school drawing teacher for twenty years, he was born in Drogobych, Poland, in 1892 and never stirred from the houses, streets, and history that informed his consciousness. His letters to a distant woman friend were the genesis of the stories not published in his books until the author was over forty. "In this way," Ficowski gently asserts, "[Schultz] alleviated his isolation without having it disturbed." Encouraged but deeply troubled by critical praise, he changed no outward circumstance of his life and the outbreak of World War II found him confined to the ghetto with the other Jews of his city. In the midst of historical juggernaut, he clung hard to everyday life and never used the false papers or money furnished him by Polish writers and underground organizations; he made no attempt to escape. A Gestapo officer who liked his drawings occasionally employed him. Armed with a special pass, Schultz was en route to the home of his "protector" on the morning of November 19, 1942, when he was shot dead outside the house by a rival officer. One-hundred-and-fifty other passersby were killed in a "limited action" that day, slaughtered to lay where they fell until nightfall, but Schultz' murder was evidently somewhat personal. "I have just killed your Jew," his murderer is said to have jeered at the windows of a fellow Nazi who valued Art over anti-Semitism. Hours later, under cover of darkness, a friend of Bruno Schultz carried his body to the Jewish cemetery and buried him.

No trace remains of that mourner, of the cemetery, or of Schultz' unpublished works, which vanished along with those who held them for safekeeping.

Do writers hate to write? I don't think so. The sense of difficulty arises from the fact that writers defy time, writing words against the erasure of things and lives. We stand in an avalanche of forgetfulness, resisting the sway of disappearance. Faced with mortality, we mourn what we might have understood and communicated, not in opinion or advice but in the delivery of a world we might have saved. Writing, we cross the divide between self and others word by word. In the very act of completing the work, we are separated from it. One way or another, the writer loses writing: the writer loses the book. Opposing oblivion, we begin to understand that language is the way in and the way out.

"Should I tell you that my room is walled up?" asks Bruno Schultz. "In what way might I leave it? Here is how: Goodwill knows no obstacle; nothing can stand before a deep desire. I have only to imagine a door, a door old and good, like in the kitchen of my childhood, with an iron latch and bolt. There is no room so walled up that it will not open with such a trusty door, if you have but the strength to insinuate it."

FRED G. LEEBRON

Not Knowing

The word *narrative* means "to know." For a long time I didn't know why I wrote. Perhaps I wrote because in an unformed desire to tell stories I had signed up for a class in writing and thus writing was required; perhaps I wrote because somebody or other told me I might get good at it if I kept doing it and so I simply kept writing to see what it would be like to be good; perhaps I wrote because as the youngest of five children it was the only way to get all the words out without somebody interrupting me. Writing seemed to be a pressure coming from outside that got transformed inside and wound up as words on the page. But mostly now I feel that it has to come from inside, that it starts inside—if sometimes in response to external events—that it is a pressure from inside to know. To find out. To see.

The word *narrative* means "to know." The reader enters the narrative to know. The character enters the narrative to know. The writer enters the narrative to know. The pressure of not knowing and wanting to know is the pressure to write, to proceed to knowledge; but it is also the pressure to read, and as well the pressure to live and breathe as a character on the page. The shared experience among writer, reader, and character is that process of discovery. If any of these participants in the process has already discovered whatever there is to be discovered, then why bother?

In Baltimore at my first graduate school I was introduced to Freytag's Triangle and taught that not only did every story need to have a beginning, middle, and end, but that every story had to have a conflict, crisis, and resolution. It was a clear model and—after my first misstep at a story, constructed as a slice-of-life family gathering at a funeral—it appeared to illuminate a path of certainty that I could trust: create a tense situation, explode it, and resolve it. Exercise absolute control of your material, pinpoint rather than approximate the meaning of every word, and you had a story. I followed this formula with an astonishing rigor. I believed in it. It kept me sane. I practiced care all the time: I was careful. I wrote careful stories of domestic trauma and affairs gone awry and absurd moments in quiet lives, stories about nuclear power plant laundries and painful miscarriages and sexualized subway incidents. When other writers tried to talk to me about the luck involved in writing a good story, I dismissed them. Writing was all craft. There was, as far as I could tell, absolutely no luck involved. I wrote story after story. I couldn't be stopped. The only weakness my teachers would point to was a possible "flaw in the imagination," evidenced by how clearly I telegraphed the ending of every story I wrote—a couple finally deciding to have a second child, a disillusioned lover fantasizing about grinding up his ex-girlfriend in a Cuisinart, a woman delicately tormented by a Dumpster diver whom she ultimately could not escape.

For years I had no idea what my strength as a writer was. I listened to everything everybody said. Was it compression, that ability to take the large and distill it to its essence? Was it plot, that capacity to realize a sequence of events and follow it through to a satisfactory conclusion? It wasn't character, apparently. Character was one of my weaknesses, one of my peers told me. And I felt and saw that, and felt it in my own character, that there was an essential weakness in it, but I didn't know what it was. But I knew my strength wasn't depth. My stories were sometimes so short and skeletal that depth could not possibly have been an element in any of them. And, as I was told often enough, my strength wasn't writing well, because anybody could write well, and if anybody could write well, then how could writing well possibly be a strength? That would be like saying eating well was a strength, or breathing well. But I knew some things about myself. I knew I had ceased to be fearless (if I ever had been), that I was more concerned about what people thought about my work than what I thought about it. I knew that in the new timidity I had ceased to be daring, to take risks, to embrace whatever was difficult or new. I kept away from exploring character interiors because I was afraid it would reveal how little I actually knew about people, that the flaw in my imagination was that I couldn't conjecture anything beyond action. I kept away from using abstractions because I was afraid it would show how little I knew about language. I wrote scene after meticulous scene, taught that dramatization was the strongest possible posture a writer could take, and read only writers who conformed to that formula. I wrote a story about a mother and a son watching a father eat a lot of candy, and I wrote a story about two brothers hanging out in a hotel room waiting for their father to die in a hospital up the road, and I wrote a story about two brothers disputing the care of their infirm mother. If I got inside anybody's head for longer than two sentences, I cut myself off. I had decided that the space inside a character's mind was by definition small and dark and tight, and anybody who spent much time in there would feel uncomfortable and oppressed. I stayed away from the inside; I exercised restraint. My stories were so restrained, so tight, that not a word or thought was loose, not a word or thought reached beyond its position on the page.

I don't know when the epiphany arrived (perhaps it still hasn't), but I know the impulses I began to hear that turned me away from the outside and back to the inside, to where the essential pressure and reason for writing breathed. One night in Iowa City I sat and listened to our instructor recount his day of writing, how he followed a character down to the basement, where he heard a strange rustling, and the character turned and drew out his gun and shot in the dumbwaiter a rat. "And," the instructor grinned, *"I didn't even know it was there."* And I thought, "So you don't have to know." I felt my mind open. It opened, but I allowed it to shut again.

One day an agent met with me in New York. "I like your stories," she said. "You need to write a novel."

I went home and made myself write a novel. A lost soul of an American narrator followed a Brazilian surfer, his girlfriend, and several other quirky characters around Peru for a series of tragicomic troubles. A year later I read the manuscript and set it aside and wrote the same novel from a Peruvian character's point of view. Then I read that version and set it aside and wrote nearly the same novel again from the Peruvian character's point of view, but in a less anguished voice. Finally I read that version and set it aside and wrote somewhat near the same novel but set in an imaginary country and told from the third-person point of view. Then—with the help of rejections from 36 publishers—I threw the novel out. I couldn't write the novel because I had been told to write the novel, and so I had sat down and made myself write a novel, I had made myself predesignate the size and shape of the work before me. I was beginning to understand that I was not the kind of writer who could do that, even if lots of wonderful writers sat down and wrote novels they knew they were going to write. But I couldn't write knowing too much. I couldn't write knowing length, and I couldn't write knowing plot, and I couldn't write knowing more than that first instant of voice. I needed not to know.

I was beginning to understand that in the larger failure of writing a weak novel I could see all the elements of failure from all my work, and these elements were born from the fact that I knew too much, that I predetermined it all, that I moved my characters like pieces on a checkerboard, that I mistakenly exercised total control, and that was what made the writing predictable and limited in all elements, from plot to voice, from character to vision. I had had no sense of the work existing beyond me. I had had no sense that—if I visited the desk every day for a period of time and allowed myself to concentrate—it could. To plot was to conjecture: There wasn't just one plot, just like there wasn't just one guess. I had to conjecture all the possible plots to know. And the not knowing, the sense of approaching and exploring understanding, would allow me the essential distance to exhaust the possibilities.

While the belovedly wretched novel was circulating among editors twenty-two through thirty-one, I began to write again. I wrote just for the fuck of it. I wrote just to see what would happen. I had a vague idea I would tell a story about my hero Nathanial West, how he moved out west to serve as a desk clerk at a low-income residential hotel, and how it had both undermined and enlightened him. To keep it loose—in other words, absolutely untied to and unconstrained by the truth—I would set it in contemporary time and in San Francisco.

Every morning I sat with a stenographer's notebook (smaller pages that would lead to less pressure to fill them) and wrote. I had about an hour each day. Usually I stole this hour on the commuter train. What the hell, it wasn't really serious; I was just writing to see. I sure as hell wasn't writing a novel, now that twenty-four, twenty-five, twenty-six editors had rejected my very first novel. I was just writing. Soon I had twenty pages, then thirty, then fifty. Uh-oh, I thought. Uh-oh, my wife thought. Everyone (including my mother) knew I couldn't write a novel. Well, so it was a long exercise. I had no idea what would happen in it from day to day. I just followed the characters. I tried not to get in the way. Sometimes what they did repulsed me, sometimes it surprised me, sometimes it disappointed me. I wanted her to kill him. She never would. I wanted him to rise up and be more of a man. He couldn't. In a year they finished whatever they were going to do together, and I was finished as well. I had a mess on my hands. It took me three years to line-edit it. But it was a novel. It was a novel in the sense that it was new to me as I wrote it, that I had no idea what would happen until it did, and that I never dictated what would happen, I just followed it, I followed it to find out.

My stories grew differently, too. I let them get out of control. I tried not to be in control, just to put pressure on the language as it pressed into the page, just to be disciplined in the sense that I would try to write every day and I would attain the same level of concentration on each day that I wrote, and just to be restrained by *not* putting myself between the world of language and the world of my characters. I used abstractions. If my characters arrived at "mercy" or "grace," I was interested in knowing exactly what they meant by that, and I followed them until they showed me. I dwelt in the interior. A teacher at Iowa who had rightfully derided me as a brand-name workshop minimalist could go fuck himself. I let sentences get out of control. I let paragraphs march along for pages. At one point my novel came back from the publisher's copy editor with the particular query: "Are you sure you want this five-page paragraph?" Yeah, I was sure. I was sure because I felt that that was what the character wanted. I just tried to want in everything I wrote what the character wanted. And all the character wanted was to know. I did, too.

Finally, as far as I was concerned, whenever I wrote I almost never wanted or needed to know. I began a longer story; perhaps it would be a novel. I wrote every day for forty-five minutes, and on days when it wouldn't come, I just sat there and stared at the wall while in the kitchen the children shrieked and my wife sighed while she waited for her turn at the desk. I followed these new characters. When they bored me or they got tired of hearing themselves think I followed other characters. I followed the point of view of a five year old and the point of view of a six month old and the points of view of two sixty-five-year-old women. I did not care what they said or thought or did as long as it was them saying or doing or thinking, and I didn't think of anybody reading it—I just thought of them doing it, and I had no idea what would happen when it did or how it would end. When the central act occurred I followed it and watched it and wrote it, and in those respects I might as well have been a journalist, covering the days of my characters, except that they offered me access to their interior worlds as well as whatever it was they felt like doing in public. When the ending came I still had doubt as to some essential truths, but I didn't care because I doubted that there ever was just one essential truth ever for anybody. One editor had written me years before that "a little ambiguity never hurt anybody," and I had read Tim O'Brien's work and decided that in ambiguity actually there was an even more essential truth. The truth of many possible and potential truths. The thread to revelation wasn't singular, it was plural, and you could follow any of a number of these threads and they all took you to one understanding or another and there was not any single understanding that was a total or an all-encompassing understanding, and that, too, became a not knowing, because you could never tell on which particular path which particular understanding would be reached until you arrived at it.

Now my writing lives in abstractions and lingers in interiors and hurtles on in overlong dialogue exchanges and I am all over the place; and here in the not knowing and the uncontrolled is a kind of victory for the writer, an essence of all pressure let loose to see what it will arrive at. Now I believe that the concept of "crisis" is the concept of loss of control, that a writer needs to lose control, to lose control of language, of voice, of plot, of character, and just follow what happens, and in that essential loss of control the prose and what you have created will transcend itself, will transcend the page, and will become as real as that familiar goal of the suspension of disbelief dictates.

Readers suspend disbelief and writers suspend disbelief because writing and reading are acts of faith along the path to knowledge, not just one particular knowledge but any knowledge that is part of the essential truths lurking to be shared by the reader and the writer and all those people in that story, that are coming not to just one conclusion but many conclusions, that follow not one path but many paths, because the writing and the story are not just about one thing but many things, and in this essential multifarious way writing is an embrace of all the complexity of not knowing and wanting to know and getting to know and all the contradictions that reside therein, and that has been our task, on these paths, all of us—writer, reader, character—to embrace those contradictions.

TOM GRIMES

If I Could Be Like Mike

I'm not sure exactly why I wanted to become a writer. Maybe it was because of my basic insecurity about mastering the act itself, the actual laying down of letters, script, my own handwriting—an identity—on paper. I scribbled terribly as a boy, eliciting the family joke, "He has a doctor's handwriting," which wasn't really a joke but more like a from-my-mouth-to-God wish of my mother's. In fact, my mother is the source of my anxiety about my penmanship and, therefore, my identity.

I repeatedly received F's on my lettering assignments when I was in third grade. Turn in a page of lowercase and capital As, get it back with an F emblazoned on it like the scarlet letter. Until, one day, a sheet covered with large and small Hs descended on my desk. At its top, the identity-validating A I'd been seeking. I bolt out of school at three P.M. No longer the worthless Dostoyevskian worm I'd felt like all my life, I wave the sheet as I run toward my mother, who's standing beside our old car, one door tied closed because the lock is broken, waiting to drive me, my sister, and my brother home.

"Slow down. What are you running for?" she says, criticizing my exuberance. What right, after all, did I have to run spontaneously?

"Look," I say, handing her the paper.

She eyes it, notes the A, and says, "Great. Who's Stanley Andro-lowitz?"

So deliriously had I been celebrating the A in my head that I didn't notice it wasn't mine. The following day I skulked back to school and exchanged Stanley Androlowitz's A for my inevitable F.

Ever since, I've fixated on my sense of being a failure waiting to be unmasked. This may be another reason why I gravitated toward writing. Over time, I felt, I could build up a body of work that might remind me, and maybe even convince the rest of the world, that I was not the weaselly little impostor bearing some-one else's A paper. Writing, scribbling sentences, I for some rea-son believed or imagined—without ever really getting to the root of why—would give me an identity I could value and esteem. Wrong!

My boyhood identity had been slapped together by the patch-work necessities, ambitions, and shortcomings of lower middle class life. My fate in the world as internist/philosopher-king had been pronounced by my mother the moment a pair of doctors wrestled all twelve-and-three-quarter pounds of me out of her womb. But, of course, my father's first Bellowesque assessment of me, "Who's that little greaseball?"—his black Irish side ill-disposed to a half-Italian firstborn who resembled Mussolini—hinted at a slight rent in the parental vision of my identity. Savior, curse.

My mother barely graduated from high school, had never learned to play an instrument as her brothers had done in order to make their livings, and with her ulcer-prone stomach somehow came up with the brilliant idea of marrying a man who disap-peared for days on benders. My father had a lousy job, an eighth-grade education, and a drinking habit that eventually got him locked up in an asylum. With my unpropitious arrival, his life of toil and paternal duty was sealed, so I understand his resentment.

My parents did what they could to raise us properly. He bought

us *The Book of Knowledge* on layaway and told me reading was the
key to all wisdom, then lay on the frayed couch and watched TV
seven nights a week. He and my mother put us through twelve
years of Catholic school. Sundays we ate roast beef after Mass,
Fridays the fish fillets my mother had overcooked until they mim-
icked the texture of bread crumbs, and at each meal silently
counted the days until I would become a doctor, my sister a nurse
or teacher, and my younger brother a janitor. Not that my parents
had any empirical basis for assigning us these respective fates
other than a few report cards, which, if anything, proved I had no
aptitude whatsoever for the hard sciences. I argued that they were
called "hard" for a reason, but my parents ignored my arguments
and waited for me to hang out my shingle. So, given that my adolescent identity had more fault lines than Southern California, it
stunned them when I announced at the dinner table one Sunday,
"I want to be a writer."

(Why are you running? Who are you to think you can write?)

My mother cried. My father told me I could go to hell, then left
the table. My mother told me to go apologize to him. Had I done
something wrong, like admit to a desire to spend my life shooting
heroin? All I'd said was, I want to be like Norman Mailer. You
think maybe it was the Jewish thing? Like I had not only abandoned medicine, but become—me, good Catholic boy, former
subscriber to *Maryknoll,* and one-time missionary wanna-be—an
infidel to boot? ("Open heart surgery will just have to wait," the
voice in my head, for some reason suddenly speaking with an
upper-class British accent, said snippily. "I have novels to write.")

By putting a book with my name on it on a shelf I would arrive,
I imagined, at a finished state of being. I'd be just like the writers I
admired—Hemingway (suicide), Fitzgerald (alcoholic), Faulkner
("No one remembers Shakespeare's children," he told his daughter when she begged him to quit drinking). Or Tolstoy (wife
despiser and frustrated grammar school teacher). Or Dostoyevsky
(compulsive gambler). With a book, I'd have an identity like my

heroes who had written powerfully but lived, in some ways, atrociously, guilty of addiction, arrogance, egomania—who knew?—maybe even bad penmanship. But they'd lived with something else too, something I wasn't able to understand at nineteen—complex identities, identities that were obviously not fixed, not put away on the shelf. Identities that, for all their flaws and mysteries, informed their written work.

Reading *The Sun Also Rises* confirmed my desire to live the life I imagined writers lived. I thought Jake Barnes had a grand life (sic!). Breakfast alone with a newspaper in a Paris cafe, five minutes at the office, two hour lunches with drinks, five minutes at the office, cocktails, dinner, more cocktails, a little fishing, a little homoerotic bonding over river-chilled wine, a little bad Spanish, some moral regeneration after a good clean well-lighted swim in Spain, then back to gay Paree for—what else?—drinks! Caught up in the delicious surface of his life, I missed the fact that the sun may also rise, but Jake's dick didn't. I also blew by the wee matter of his profession. He went out so much because he was a journalist, not a novelist!

Novelists sit in small lonely rooms three to five hours a day, exhilarated when we hit a slight groove, which may only be fifty words in a row, four to five handwritten lines on a notebook page. For me, this comes, if it comes, deep into the writing day, well after the initial what-is-this-about, who-wrote-this phase, the ritual confusion and shame that hits me each time I flip open to the page I've left incomplete the day before. Then, because I listen to music when I write, I'll get into a song and forget about the book for a while. Soon I may notice a word that could be exchanged for a word that captures all the nuances and rhythms I want, and I'll erase the first one and test the new one, weighing it, running the new sentence through my head to see how it sounds. By then, the music coming through my headphones has given way to the book's music, which takes me with it until finally I'm in two places, at my desk and in the book's world. Athletes call this being in the zone. If you're hitting a baseball, each pitch seems to come in slow motion, the ball the size of a grapefruit. If you're shooting hoops, the basket is suddenly the size of a Jacuzzi. You see the whole game, almost from someplace outside of your body. This is what it feels like to hit the groove. Only some days, no groove. Some days, the book that's working on me (it isn't the other way around) won't let me in. My shot's off, my timing's bad. And, of course, it's my fault.

What should I do, take a day off? If I do, will I lose the thread? If I take a day off, might I never come back to the book? Novelists never get vacations, we don't have deadlines, and we can't be fired. But we can quit. I've quit four times, convinced that my work was irredeemably bad. (And I'm still not sure it isn't.) But each time I quit I come back, usually in the form of scribbling, just a few words scratched onto a stray sheet of paper. Then something magnetic in the words reaches out, drawing more words out of me, the words themselves slowly beginning to insist upon extension, examination, explication, completion. I never know what completion will consist of, much less read like, but I'm in a zone now and can't pull out. This force field tugs me into a novel. I don't know what I'm doing, but I'm trusting the words, for only words can temporarily assuage the near perpetual doubt novelists live with, the revulsion for the work that sets in, as Beckett said, the instant the ink dries.

Roth talks about writing pages and pages, then scouring them for a single line with vitality, some life, the force field I'm talking about, that might be the beginning of a book. Once I tap into that, I'm gone. The high of being in the middle of a novel is my only true period of identity, not happiness but identity, being full with the book, pregnant with it. But, as Roth also says, a period of hating the book follows.

Hating a book comes because novelists never get it completely right. We always miss, by a hairsbreadth if we're lucky, worse if we're not, the vision we've chased Ahab-like for years. I once described trying to complete my third novel as flying a 747 in a blizzard when the fuel gauge is on empty, the cockpit windows blown out, two engines sheared off, and the ghost of all of litera-ture is standing over my shoulder, gun at my head, shouting at me like a terrorist to land the fucker! (Novelists can be prone to grandiose overstatement.) I'd seen the climactic scene of the novel in my mind two years before I wrote it. Just a brief flash in, of all places, Wichita, while driving on I–35, my wife asleep beside me. A buzz shot through me. I saw two characters, one with his hand outstretched, and this was the magnetic force that drew me forward, everything in the book moving toward that image.

Pressure builds as you approach the end of a novel. Unlike short stories, the chances are not that you will make a sudden wrong move and wreck everything. With novels, the likelihood is more that you won't get everything in, won't catch every possible echo and reverberation. I'm always afraid that I won't, for some reason, squeeze all the juice out of the lemon. So as I hurtle toward closure, I need to slow down at the same time. I desper-ately want the book to end; I never want the book to end. I'm ter-rified and ecstatic. When I wrote the end of that closing chapter I literally dropped my pencil, sat up straight, and raised my fists in the air.

Because I'd always assumed that I'd never write anything worth a damn (and I have plenty of proof in boxes), and because the zone I'd been entering daily for three years has suddenly broken like a fever, I lose it when I finish a novel. I finished my second thinking I had three hundred more pages to write. I stood up, looked at the clock, saw I'd put my four hours in, so I thought, I'll quit for the day, the hard part's over. I know where the book has to go. Then I realized I could end it—immediately. I sat down, wrote out the final paragraph, then I started crying like a maniac. When I called my wife Jody at work to tell her, she thought I was trying to say I was leaving or the cats were dead or I had seven brain tumors or something that to the non-irrational might be worthy of complete emotional breakdown.

When this stage passes I revise with terrific energy until, finally, five pages from the end of the fourth full revision when I'm arguing with Jody, who edits, over where a comma should go, and fuck and goddammit and Jesus Christ have come to constitute my entire vocabulary, I say, "Why are we fighting over a sentence? The whole book is a disaster!" Then the answer is suddenly clear to me—I've been insane for three years and these are my notes from underground! Now, and only now, when I'm convinced the book is an utterly misbegotten debacle, do I give in, say it's done, and decide to get, as the saying goes, professional help.

Novels exhaust us, Robert Stone once said somewhere. They beat us. And he's right. Plus, once we've lost, they continue to mystify us.

Sitting in a bar one night after workshop, the novel I had come to Iowa to write completed only days earlier, I said to Frank Conroy, "I feel like a ghost. It's like Mike," my book's first-person narrator, not Michael Jordan, "left my body and I don't know who I am anymore. It's like I was him and now he's gone."

Looking at me with some surprise, Frank said, "You're nothing like him."

This is two grown guys sitting around—over drinks anyway, score one for Jake Barnes!—comparing my flesh-and-blood identity to a fictive pastiche of common American boyhood traits, an identity composed of paper, ink, and words, words, words. Maybe this is why my mother cried when I said the W word—writer. "Hi, this is my son. He makes things up instead of curing leukemia." She still calls to tell me who in the family is terminally ill, as if it's my fault. "A novel," she says to me, "is that fiction or nonfiction?" What am I, writing prescriptions? How do I know? I can't even tell who's me and who the character I invented is!

"I'm not?" I say to Frank.

"Not at all."

"Man."

He laughed, then said, "Hey, the illusion worked. That's what it's supposed to do."

Fine. But what happens to me when the illusion vanishes, when the book wears me out and skips off to be pampered by some loving proofreader who niggles away at all the tiny flaws I've left behind to deface an otherwise perfect story, my every literary shortcoming noted, every long sentence with too many dashes and ellipses and—what else?—triple metaphors that test the patience of readers like show-offy kids because they slow a story down till it's moving like a supermarket checkout line and make reviewers want to yell like the movie directors they wish they were—"Cut!"—every bit of narrative exuberance condemned as "self indulgent." (They should only know I don't know who I am, so how can I indulge myself?!) And while the book has marketing people cooing over it (until the day it's born and bombs) and artists designing its cover and everybody in the house and every would-be buyer gets to handle it, where am I? At home night-sweating how much better the book could have been, despairing over missed opportunities, insights that came too late, wisdom deferred.

When the book arrives it goes, unread, directly onto the bookshelf where I always thought I wanted it (the Chinese curse—you get what you wish), staring out at me from its snug spot amidst the spines of books authored by my literary idols whose work, whose names, always appear to me somehow more fixed, solid, more like they're attached to an identity than mine. These other writers have accomplished something—they've written books. Me? Impostor that I am, I've somehow pulled a fast one on the literary world. But at any moment the covers of my books are going to peel away and I'll see, without the aid of hallucinogenics, just my own identity troubled, perhaps chemically imbalanced—what? Self? What me is there? Like Pynchon's *V*, I'm not a who. Who I'll deal with later. First I want to know what I am—and this whatness knows that when the covers of my books are stripped away there will be, embossed in gold leaf on a beautiful linen spine (I wish)—what else?—Stanley Androlowitz! Not because I haven't written the books, but because I don't know who or what

I am when I'm not writing books. The act that as a nineteen-year-old boy I imagined would bestow identity upon me has instead, like some trickster, doubled my identity troubles. I'm a doppelganger of characters who don't exist!

Yet I feel every day I don't write is wasted. "Not only are your books not up to snuff, you're not writing them fast enough," the voice in my head tells me. You drink too much, you don't drink enough. Loosen up, buckle down. Who ever told you that you could be a writer? What are you running for? I feel lousy about not writing books that no one asked me to write, and if I ever do write them, I'll feel guilty for not writing them well enough!

Is this what fiction has done to me? Philip Roth's character David Kepesh wonders after he has metamorphosed into a giant breast. Have I, at the identity level, likewise been deformed by writing? Would I know myself any better had I found the cure for cancer and was headed for the Royal Swedish Academy to accept a Nobel in medicine instead of scribbling? "And the Nobel for worst penmanship goes to …" Or would I have been just as puzzled about that squiggly blob of mercury I still want to call my identity?

Roth talks about the elusiveness of identity, how writing in the first person, conjuring up the illusion of an identity that is ostensibly "me," might be the subtlest, most complicated illusion of all. Great. Not only have I picked the wrong profession, but I picked the one least likely to give me a clear, firm sense of self.

No one ever told me to become a writer; I blame myself. But if all writers are readers moved to emulation, then maybe all of literature urged me to write. Maybe what I've wanted all along was what Tolstoy and Hemingway and DeLillo seem to have, which turns out, upon close reading, not to be identity but negative capability, that mysterious Keatsian ability and desire to swim through confusion and, without anxiously or irritably grasping after facts (those tempting, untranscendent things), keep themselves afloat. Maybe I'd misread my longing to be a writer, just as

Harold Bloom says all fledgling writers misread the work of their strong predecessors in order to join their ranks. Maybe I mistook being a writer as an end, a place of arrival, when what I really wanted, what I was really searching for, was not identity but mystery, reflection, doubt, a constant state of never knowing who I am, always testing, always weighing, always evolving. And I find this testing ground in notebooks on the pages of which I scrawl my As and Fs, the cave drawings of my soul, the script that gradually reveals to me who and what I am—unfinished, no terminus in sight until the grave, and even then, who knows?

BARRY HANNAH

Mr. Brain, He Want a Song

Ah well, the brain wants a song. And the message is always the same—we are alive and dying. Hot wind in the skull. No possum, no sop, no taters until we sing the song. You have to act or not eat. Sing the song, then fall on your victuals, and become a man. Otherwise you are a half-man, a zombie, an uninvited guest, if you feel like me when I can't sing. This might go on for months. Food is bitter and friends are flat.

It has been said we might all write better under tyranny. This could be true of white Americans at the end of the century. Sometimes it seems to me we are obscenely self-conscious and all talked-out. Nothing presses us and we are lost in the absolute freedom of jabber. "My rhetoric ain't gonna be like nobody's rhetoric, Jack. 'Cause I got this fey morphodike point of view." Others turning sick simply because they are tired of themselves. Yet Mr. Brain, he sick of sickness. He want a song, Jack.

May I suggest that writing itself is freedom from consciousness as much as a stimulant to it. That writers are not always the most vital people in the room, but often nearer ghouls sniffing at the trough of other living blood. That they are malingering vampires who never got the hang of life, really. That they are narcoleptics so enchanted by their inner dreams that only the act of writing itself can shake them into sullen awareness, and then they sleep again, having stolen something from the house of old chaos and time. Writing has saved the soul once more from the insufferable war of full consciousness. For a time. He has put himself in that beloved trance again. Possum, sop, taters.

I would guess this is why I find working writers to be among the happiest folks in the world. Among the unhappiest are those who are not working and have endless questions. You do not want to get within a block of these people. The Great Suck—big bottom lip, the sulk, the neurotic and despondent vortex. But working writers are happy like unprosecuted felons.

Now let me insist these are *good* vampires and ghouls and felons, lovely boys and girls for the most part, generous and helpful once awake and clued-in. They are some of the best *teachers* in the world. With their itching and inching work at home, they can explain what happens on the page much better than their colleagues, who are likely to be theorists of literature who can neither read nor write and are apt to pronounce on every work of the imagination as if it were a mere psychosocial tract. They have kept the blood in writing and have invited the young into the world of literature *just to have a touch of it,* as opposed to the gasses of the professoriate, who are not just beyond the pale but *are* the pale. It is no wonder the writing schools are overcrowded and very handsome marketable programs at many schools today. Some have lamented that we are losing our best readers to the writing schools. That more should be content *just* to read. But on the other hand, it is a desperation of the sane, who want to be at least *close* to the source in these days of "texts" and further tertiary bullshit.

On my recent visit to the famous Iowa Writers' Workshop, where the writing was of a high order, by students from the best schools in the land, I was impressed by how many of them, unbidden, told me what wonderful teachers they had. There was a measurable thrill in the classrooms, as in the old days, and I pray God I did my part in it. My ideal has been, since his early death in 1982, the irreplaceable Richard Hugo. What a spirit, as firm as a statue around the precincts of Missoula, Montana, as palpable as that of William Faulkner in my own town of Oxford. Hugo was a great poet, a brilliant reader (hands behind his back, reciting his poems without text from his big yearning belly—a miracle!), a victor over depression, and a teacher who could bring tears to the eyes of the strong when he explained the righteous knowing of poetry. The last good kiss in a bankrupt gray-skied Montana hamlet. My word, I feel so lucky to have known him, even briefly. Marvin Bell told me when he met Hugo the first time, the poet sat down and straightaway declared, "You know, I don't have much luck with women." That was Hugo, his soul in his mouth. The first time I met him at the university, he said, "Welcome, Barry. You'll be a real shot in the arm for these kids." I was so gratified to hear this I grew instantly serious about my task, and have been since. This was Hugo: In the land of very solemn High Church fly fishermen, he fished from a Buick convertible, with worms and lead, while swing music played from the tape deck. His memorial service was a salvo of testimony from PhDs, old cronies from the Seattle ship-yard and Boeing and fellow writers drunk and sober. A sweet and guilty soul, of withering honesty and intelligence, Hugo still leads my way when I enter that half-depressed funk many of us do right before teaching a class. Or when I have started a story every way but the honest one and finally find my way to it, hearing Hugo's voice in the immortal Letter poems.

The brain needs a song. The other night I dreamed a scene of pickled eggs in a massive jar at the end of a dark-wooded gold-wrapped bar, immense. I wanted two boiled and salted eggs very badly, and then a cold beer, "Very yellow if you will," I asked the barman. I'd never said anything like that in my waking life, and in my waking life I've not had a drink of anything alcoholic in nine years. The eggs were superb, salt on their skin and the pickle brine in them, and the beer better than any I'd ever tasted, cold, hoppy, barley-wild gold down my throat into all the creeks of my belly.

The experience was so intense I am still awed by the dream, can still taste the beer. The dream has little meaning beyond this intensity, as far as I can tell. I am still refreshed by the intensity. Many of my stories begin like this. A break out of consciousness into dream, a song of an egg and a beer.

I come from a land, the South, with much religion, and as far as I can tell, zero philosophy, which suits me fine. Philosophy, except as it is expressed in bursts of song, poems, and stories, has never gripped me, although I wanted badly once to be an existentialist, but mainly for the beret, turtleneck, cigarettes, and wan chick across the table listening. I have never been interested in what makes a writer a writer or the "creative process." I met an old friend, a fine trumpet man, in Seattle a couple of years ago, who told me he was very interested in the "creative process." I recall getting angry, angrier than I'd have predicted of myself. What in hell for? I asked him. I would guess that one's childhood would have more to do with bank theft than writing. Don't give me this "alienation" yammer. Writers come from both spoiled and depraved lives. The well-groomed square will often outwrite the professional hippie, and I have witnessed the unsettling fact that fine novels come from men and women with so little personality they are not even annoying. Samuel Beckett told many people that he had perfect memories of himself as a foetus in a dark and painful place, hearing the voices of dinnertime outside. He told Harold Pinter that the only form in his work was that of a scream. Yet these facts could supply the main biography of any random lunatic who can't even make a statement in finger painting.

The brain needs a song. In my case, with my training in poetry (failed Beat poet) and music (failed jazz trumpet) and sports (failed small quarterback, now mere tennis wimp), what is required is the intense image. If the image is intense enough, in life or in dream, it always brings a narrative with it. Without the intense image my work dwindles quickly into dishonest and empty sentences. But I don't know why this should be greatly instructive to anybody else. Good writers work from characters, and even, gasp, story itself. The rich ones seem, all, to be good at plot, and will explain plot as the obvious and only motive, and quite glibly, as if there need be no argument through the ages on this matter. Too much concern for process is the very awareness you are escaping when you write—the gnawing, niggling world. I believe, after a certain point, it is not good to read too many books. I will go even further and suggest that it is not good for a writer to know too much history, since he is making it, presumably. I go along with Henry Ford, who said history is bunk. I wrote best when I barely knew who was president.

You want joy and respect, of course, even aristocracy. Rich in friends, pride in the bank, a good name. Not to be called Bozo. Things like that. I do not think process is interesting, but I believe what brought a writer to the table might be. For me, that would be romance, big and little letters, failure, and the pissed-off conviction that almost everybody of my era had gotten everything wrong. I even took pride, eventually, in being from one of the most derided states in the union, Mississippi, which was then essentially South Africa, wherein all organs of print, teachers, and preachers assured us daily that things were just dandy. I played jazz trumpet fairly well, but then Elvis broke out—this white-trash mama's boy; we all knew his type in every school—and condemned the horn to baleful irrelevance for thirty years. My English teacher, Lois Blackwell, when I was a sad reeling seventeen, began commenting pretty passionately about my poems and I began listening to her. Mrs. Blackwell was a nice-looking blonde fired from church organ for smoking, who knew French, jazz, Dinah Washington, and Edith Piaf. I got the feeling she had been at New York parties with Tennessee Williams. Her brother was an eminent English litera- ture scholar and morphine addict, which, since I was Beat, sounded flat-out heroic to me, especially as he scholared away in some jerkwater Mississippi town with slick Negroes (the form pre- ferred by us aristocrats) fetching him dope. Then Mrs. Blackwell played Dylan Thomas on the phono. Romance, baby. God, to be Welsh and drunk and start hollering out surrealism. Romance, my angel-headed hipsters! Poetry! Imagine the solemn beauties all at you in those New York parties!

That summer I met an alarming woman in a cemetery across the reservoir from our cabin, where we vacationed. There was a cedar grove around the cemetery and wild irises of all colors near an iron gate standing alone, no fence. It was cool here, in hot July. I had a canoe with an electric trolling motor on it, borrowed from the odd professor in the next cabin who thought UFOs sat down to take on water from the reservoir. The woman sat on a grave, where I walked up to her. The fourth time I visited her, she had a little dog named Face with her, a corgi and beagle mix. She wanted me to take the dog away because her husband might kill it, knowing she loved it so much. He was an old man with old friends who came over to trouble her. She told me the whole county wanted to make her pregnant. I'd guess she was around twenty-two or so. She had some typewritten pages in her lap, and some pictures of herself as a younger girl. I agreed she was very pretty in every picture and even better now. She brought out a half-smoked pack of Oasis cigarettes and told me she wanted me to take these, too. But I didn't smoke. No, for *me*, to remember me by my brand of smoke. Her husband and his friends would tear up her poems and her pictures and didn't allow her to smoke at all. She said things had got dangerous, even *final*.

I was somewhat scared of her, scared of her life, which thrilled me. She once wanted to show me the edge of her house that you could see from the next hill, but I didn't want to see it. Now she read a couple of her poems. She took a long time with them, and I could not imagine how she could get this length out of the short amount of typing on the page. I think they sort of jangled like the lines of Poe. With some passion she wrapped the pictures and the cigarette pack in the typed sheets and folded them where I could get them in my shirt pocket.

Then, as before, she bared her bosoms. She wore a brassiere with a flower clasp in front. They were fine, freckled at the top. In memory, however, I see them as so lonesome and pathetic, ground over by old time and chaos, that I could weep. The irises and the cedars and the iron gate, cool green with these ghosts, her breasts, in them, floating away already. I asked her why she married the old man. She told me he was the only one worth marrying in the county. I asked weren't there other counties? I doubt it, she said.

On the reservoir with the dog Face in the canoe, I drove homeward, but the water went dark, and big lightning started. I was out a mile in the center. The waves rose and began getting very white. The electric motor could make no progress. The canoe was swept around so it almost washed over every time a bigger wave struck. The dog was scratching me in nearly rabid fear. I was trying to reattach a battery cable when Face took this chance to jump out of my arms and swim for home. Even in this storm, I was thinking home for him was death. He was really getting out there with his head high, as if he'd done this many times. A nearly opaque white rain came on. I jumped after the dog and began swimming, luckily, with the big waves. My face was underwater everywhere and it was a problem breathing. But I was set on the dog and don't remember much fear. I finally caught him. A treetop stood out of the water, and I caught it. The dog scratched me badly again, but I hung on for us both. Finally my legs and arms were gone, and I fell asleep.

I woke up to the sound of a regular bass boat engine. It was the professor, and he was very angry. He was towing the canoe, but the motor and battery had been dumped out of it. Further, he despised dogs. What the hell kind of kid are you? he accused me. I supposed you were a man.

My mother and father never understood about the dog, and looked at it as if it were an unwelcome mystery for a while. Worse, my mother discovered the poems, all water-melted around the pictures and cigarettes, when she did the laundry. When I spread out the poems on my desk they had gaps in them. Everafter ... nacreous ... gaping ... seed. It suddenly shot through me that this was romance, and I had had it. I was frightened and illicit and sullen. This was where the action was. Frightened, illicit, sullen. Art! Even stammering art, accidental art. The woman, the bosoms, the dog handy to hand, the wracked poems. The idea of the poems, more than content or meaning! That's it! I was in the middle, I was an invited guest! *Dangerous, final,* she'd said. Oh life! The first hit of art is a kick, like junk. But William Burroughs explains patiently that junk is not a kick. It is a way of life.

So soon, a few years hence, married too early and miserable in all ways, having fled from my parents for freedom and got hogtied in the worst slavery, I had a job in pharmacology, injecting poor dogs with nerve gas from the Army (we didn't know what it was) in a sealed-off section fourth floor of the medical school in Jackson. The dogs did not die, thank God, but were incapacitated. I took notes on respiration, heart rate, and pinprick sensitivity in the extremities and lumbar region. The logbook was a handsome thing, bound in fake leather with gold stripes running through oxblood borders. I wore a white coat, and my duties were not crushing. I waited for the dog to get better, mainly, and petted it, after injecting the stuff into its femoral artery. I began liking the logs very much, and stole them. I am not a stealing man, not at all. But this was my art. In my white coat, having conquered mere adulthood and manhood in my time—that is, doing something miserable and nasty for money—I moved on desperately to my art. I have alleged training in poetry, but I had no real training. I just wanted the intense images, the life. I had no stories to tell; my poems simply got longer and longer. I recall the stolen lab records, the Scripto pen, which went elegantly and slowly on the green-lined pages, and the stolen English Oval cigarettes, which in my poverty (Oh Life!) I hooked from the fancy tumbler on the desk of the department head. I still have the books on my shelf, not daring to look into my young wretchedness. It doesn't matter what they mean or say. It simply matters that the poems are in there, all of them yearning to be stories, among the earnest notations on dog behavior (without variance every dog shat out his all) under nerve gas injection. I am not nostalgic or that much ego-driven, for that matter. Someday I'll look at the books again. But the main thing was theft; I was stealing time. Illicit, frightening, exquisite freedom from consciousness. In fact, I believe I saved myself by way of the bad poems. It was always life intense I was after, life as its own comment when drawn well enough, never much else.

So I like these things declared by the masters:

Miles Davis, interrupting an interviewer: "Hold on. My music never had nothing to say about *life.*" His music *was* life.

Jackson Pollack: "I don't paint nature. I *am* nature."

The brain wants a song. You steal it, and then you smile a while, hoping it will stand, for your friends and even enemies, while we are alive and dying.

Now I go to my film idols, men whose deaths have changed my world into a sadder one. William Holden. Burt Lancaster. Montgomery Clift.

I don't recall a word they ever said. But I sure as hell remember how they *were.*

I would go to them for the ideal power I expect from art, even very meekly and frighteningly my own. The power beyond words themselves. And hope it might be said that my work, too, was remarkable life.

SUSAN POWER

The Wise Fool

I am sometimes invited to visit colleges (and on rare occasions, high schools) to talk about the writing process and life as a writer. The question I am asked most often is: What launched *The Grass Dancer* (my first novel)? With what feels like a mischievous smile I reply quite honestly: "Drugs." The students always laugh, in surprise (gratitude?). The teacher who is hosting me is still smiling when I glance at him, but I can practically hear his thoughts, *My God, we're paying her good money to encourage these kids to...* Before he can complete the sentence I've imagined forming in his stunned mind, I quickly explain. You see, several years ago I was a student at the Iowa Writers' Workshop and woke up one morning in terrible pain. I ended up having an emergency appendectomy and spent nearly a week in the hospital, sleepy with morphine. During those lost days of thick sleep, garbled conversations, and groggy confusion, an image came to me. I saw a Dakota woman, wearing a beautiful buckskin dress, which was completely beaded across the yoke. The cut beads sparkled even more than is usual, and the effect was quite dazzling. The woman was moving, never static, so I looked down at her feet and realized she was dancing. Peering more closely I noticed she was not gliding across the hospital floor but was forming her graceful steps on the surface of the moon, which I knew was somewhere outside my curtained room, and yet was unaccountably present inside as well. Just days before the unexpected surgery, I had volunteered a story to the fiction workshop I was taking that semester and upon release from the hospital had only a week to write something new to hand in for class. I could have submitted an old story, but I prided myself on always having fresh material. I was casting around for ideas—what to write?—when I suddenly remembered the odd vision from my sickroom. What *was* that beautiful woman doing dancing on the moon? Who was she? In order to satisfy my own curiosity I wrote her story, a piece eventually titled "Moonwalk." The woman was a dying grandmother named Margaret Many Wounds, and she was having an adventure she shared with her grandson, Harley, and (thankfully) with me. After writing the story I had the sinking feeling that it was merely a section of what would ultimately be a larger work. I had launched a novel, having no real idea of how to go about such business. I need not have worried. My characters guided me through the process.

I have tried to write this essay several times, and have given up the formal voice I so longed to adopt for this piece, written for a teacher I greatly admire. I realize that I have no characters to keep me company on these pages, no hidden secrets to uncover, and so it is a trickier undertaking for me than the channels of plot I usually ride. The only way I can tell you about writing and what has helped me to do what I do is to tell you a story, because otherwise I would feel too much as if I were back in school, cranky and inattentive. I will tell you that writing is my great adventure. There is a tarot card in the Albano-Waite deck that comes immediately to mind when I think of writing. It is the first card in the set, number zero, and is called simply The Fool. Pictured is a beautiful young man with bright blond hair, the color of daisies. He is walking briskly, excitedly, a small pack slung over his shoulder—he travels light, one has to when one is as impulsive as this fellow. His only companion is a small dog, leaping joyously at his feet, looking up at the young man with great affection. Neither of them is aware of what stands directly before him. They are so eager to be off, to see the world, to explore, they haven't noticed that they are nearing the edge of a cliff. Interestingly enough, this card is not considered negative—unless it appears upside down in a reading, or in the company of other, more ominous cards. It represents the intoxicating risk of a new beginning, a naive faith in oneself, a sense of optimism. This is where I place myself when I write. I am the Fool, about to step off the edge of the world, unafraid of the fall. If I were to look down I would stop myself, and perhaps it would be safer to remain there, on the flat green field, but from that position the view would always be the same.

This is really the story of a grump. It's true I like to leap off cliffs in summoning words from the deep places within myself, but it's also true I don't like anyone looking over my shoulder as I do this, telling me how to go about it. I smile to myself, amused, confounded, whenever I am audience to an established writer who sets forth the rules, the commandments of literature. "THOU SHALT NOT ..." Whenever I am told I should *not* do something, it is, of course, the very thing I want to do next. This is the same writer who will go on to declare what one must *always* do. "THOU SHALT ..." There will be none of that here, for perhaps you are a grump like me. I have distilled the rules and come up with one, just one, I feel can fit all of us: You should find what works best for you. Some writers must write every day, some need more thinking time. I have made considerable leaps as a writer from the production of one story to the next, with months between the writing of the two. The difference was not that I was writing, writing, writing every day, but that I had read perhaps three incredible novels in the intervening weeks. My process is not that of the mason who builds slowly and carefully, but that of a slumbering volcano, subject to periodic fiery convulsions. I have, however, come to accept that writing is not the fey party I once imagined it to be, but a great deal of work. I blame it on my characters because they take me places I would sometimes rather not go. They have careers or hobbies I know absolutely nothing about, or live in places, times, I have not experienced firsthand, so I am forced to do research.

I spend a lot of time searching for the truth of my fiction. I used to imagine myself as the great God of my work, the Bringer of Life, the Grim Reaper, the all-knowing, all-powerful, Almighty hand. After all, where would my characters be without me? They wouldn't exist. No one would ever meet them or come to care about them. They would never do the things I made them do. But then I came to realize that in order to find the truth of their stories, their experiences, I could not simply work my will upon them. I had to discover what the *real* stories were, the *actual* circumstances. I am still talking about invention, of course, this world of fiction, exercising the imagination like another muscle of the body. But I contend that in the best fiction there is no room for multiple endings, for several options, for five answers to one question. There is only one way a fictional event could possibly happen, a single solution to dilemmas of plot: the truth. The challenge for me is finding my way to that truth. Here again, I enlist the aid of my characters. Sometimes they are voluble, noisy with answers, while other times I am forced to work harder to learn their histories, understand their situation. There have been occasions when I have developed a plot before taking the time to develop the characters, needing then to completely alter a story line to fit what I later comprehend of the parties involved. Some of my characters balk at the things I would have them do, and I must respect their integrity, listen to them, and revise the text accordingly. I had *such* plans for one young man, Thomas Iron Star, a seventeen-year-old Dakota character who attends the Carlisle Indian Industrial School in 1890. I imagined that when he spends a summer on a farm in Vermont with a white family who is eager to teach him how to be "civilized" (an actual school program at the time), he would fall in love with fourteen-year-old Abigail, a member of the family. But in the end, in writing the chapter, Thomas would not cooperate. I could certainly put down the words, make him say or do anything I wanted. Yet none of it sounded right. I could tell this was the wrong approach, the wrong conception of the relationship between Thomas and Abigail. I had to reimagine the plot of a large section of the novel. Another character, a woman named Columbia, gives birth to a child I know she is destined not to raise. Yet how does she lose custody of her child? Who claims him? What happens to him? I could come up with several possible scenarios, but none of them felt accurate. I was stumped for a long time. I could not move forward until I knew the story of what happened to Columbia's son. I resorted to a strategy I use when I am most desperate: I interview my characters. I sit down at the keyboard and pelt them with questions, free-writing a response in their voice. I begin with easy questions: What is their favorite color? What images or associations does the shade summon to mind? Silly things to find my way into their voice. A harder question I usually save for later in the exercise is, what do you most fear? I nearly always come up with an interesting, revelatory response. If I am having a difficulty with plot, I ask the character about it towards the end of the interview, and if I am lucky, they tell me the story straightaway. Columbia, however, was not able to "tell" me when I asked her. The memory was too painful, I think. I didn't find the truth and solve the problem until I went to another source—the child's father. When I interviewed him I didn't yet know who he was, what his background was, how he had met Columbia. He gave me the information I needed without hesitation.

With all this talk of the writer as God, you would think I equated the ego with writing, or at least, with the product of one's labors. This is not the case. I think of the ego as an enemy of good fiction, a troublemaker. The ego watches itself in the mirror, poses and admires itself, evaluates, criticizes, is entirely too self-conscious, self-absorbed. I try to distract the ego when I write, or lock her up in some part of me and not let her out until I'm finished for the day. In high school I had a marvelous acting teacher who reminded us that when we were onstage in a performance we should be ever mindful of our characters' motivation, what their concerns are from moment to moment. She discouraged us from pulling back from the character in order to evaluate ourselves as we performed. She told us not to "watch" ourselves. She said that if we were onstage thinking, "Hmm, wasn't that an elegant gesture, so natural, so inspired, the audience will surely appreciate this performance ..." we would no longer be acting. We would no longer be artists practicing our craft. She taught us to set the audience aside when we performed, they were never central to the action, and to set ourselves aside. I now attempt to apply this strategy to my writing, to place myself in the work, focused so firmly on the world of my fiction, the events, the players, I don't have remaining energy to look over my shoulder. I tell myself I can worry about audience and revision after I have gotten something down, after I've gone to that other place of craft and imagination, inspiration. In my most unkind moments I think of the ego as "the big dummy," the lumbering creature I must push out of the way so that I can have clear access to the far more refined, fascinating, and fascinated part of my brain, the mysterious subconscious. We understand so little about the creative process, it requires a kind of faith to give oneself up to the system. In my experience, writing is a blind faith. I trust that help will come eventually if I persist in my curiosity, my investigation. If I look, and then look again, at a situation I've envisioned, in time I will understand what it all means, or at least, what I *think* it means. In time I will be able to translate this vision so that others can see what I am seeing.

Nearly every writer has been given the advice, "Write what you know." This seems to me to rely too heavily on the narrow, limited ego and conscious mind I've already slandered. I prefer another piece of advice I have heard, "Write what you need to know." If I were to concentrate solely on the material I had experienced firsthand, I would keep to my journal and never attempt to imagine myself in another's shoes. In fiction I can wear several hats: I can fight battles, give birth to children, work magic, walk the earth as a ghost. In fiction there is nothing I cannot do, there are no boundaries, there are no rules (except to somehow make it work). In fiction there are endless possibilities, roads leading in every direction. In fiction there is always the chance to start over, to take back what was said and unsay it, to change the ending. I can't think of a more exciting adventure.

When I was a little girl my father would read to me each night, even after I was able to read for myself. His voice was rich with variety, dramatic and urgent, captivating. To this day I am convinced that the best writing should be read aloud, savored, tasted, each word a necessary word, the only one that will do. I "discovered" Shakespeare when I was about ten years old, was spelled to awe by the lively tumult of his words, the lush rain of English that poured across me when I listened to his plays on records borrowed from the library. I didn't catch all the references, mine was the most inexpert admiration, yet I knew we were related across continents and time in our love for this trickster language. When I write it is not just my hand against the page or my fingers tapping keys, but an oral work. I must listen to myself in order to hear the odd rhythm, the awkward phrase that throws a sentence off-balance. Not only do I edit the text by reading it aloud, I take it a step further by audiotaping a story or chapter so that I can focus entirely on the sound of my language, its music or noise, its sense or clumsy disorder. There is nothing I will not do to spin this straw into gold.

I am an intuitive writer, absorbing technique through a constant diet of reading, not wanting to analyze too closely the mysteries of this process, afraid perhaps of finding the humbug of a little man behind the ferocious mask of Oz. There is a reverence I feel for this calling; it is like a religion to me with its secrets and rituals, its gifts. I am both the God of my work and its Fool, the colorful jester whose presence is suffered by the court because he is entertaining—society's most dangerous, most necessary critic, living somewhere outside the stream of ordinary life, the detached observer.

For the longest time I could not reconcile the two contrasting images I had of myself as a writer. Was I really the God of my fictional world, the literal Creator who dispensed life with one hand, only to snatch it away with the other? Or was I the unobtrusive observer, in service to my characters and my words, increasingly skilled at getting out of the way? I understand now that I am both: the benevolent God who gives life to men and women who interest me, brings them into this world with gifts and challenges, desires and dreams, frailties. But I am not an interfering God. I will let them make their own mistakes, exercise free will. I will imagine them into being, introduce them to one another, set them in motion. Then they will live their stories and I will tell them.

MARGOT LIVESEY

The Hidden Machinery

The personality of the writer does become important after we have read his book and begin to study it. When the glamour of creation ceases, when the leaves of the divine tree are silent, when the co-partnership (between writer and reader) is over, then a book changes its nature, and we can ask ourselves questions about it such as "What is the author's name?" "Where did he live?" "Was he married?" "Which was his favourite flower?" ... Study is only a serious form of gossip.

E.M. Forster, "Anonymity: An Inquiry," 1925

I

Percy, the Bad Chick

On the bookshelves of my house in London are the books I read as a child: Robert Louis Stevenson's *Kidnapped*, Kenneth Grahame's *The Wind in the Willows*, Lewis Carroll's *Alice's Adventures in Wonderland*, George MacDonald's *The Princess and Curdie*, and a strange book called *The Pheasant Shoots Back* by Dacre Baldson. This last, an account of how a family of pheasants outwitted the hunters and lived to fly another season, was thought by my great aunt Jean a suitable gift for my fifth birthday. Certainly I appreciated the sky-blue cover and the simple line drawings, but the black marks that covered the pages were a mystery and not one I was eager to solve. Reading struck me as much less important than tree-climbing or bridge-building. Some time that autumn, however, my priorities shifted. I remember standing in the corner, staring at a page, refusing to read, and then, quite suddenly, the black marks disappeared, leaving in their stead the story of "Percy, The Bad Chick." I emerged from the corner and read with gusto the tale of the rebellious chick who overcomes his more decorous peers and rises to power in the farmyard. From then on I embraced books, and those books, although the word remained unknown to me for several more years, were novels.

At the University of York I studied English and philosophy, which meant beginning with Chaucer and reading erratically forward until we reached D.H. Lawrence, when we came to an abrupt halt. One faculty member was rumoured to be working on a living author, the Australian novelist Patrick White, but that was a private activity; he lectured on the safely interred Eliot, Pound, and Woolf. Nonetheless news reached me from the larger world that there were people— Saul Bellow, Margaret Drabble, Doris Lessing—living, breathing, making novels now and making them out of the fabric of contemporary life. So when I went traveling the year after university, writing a novel seemed the obvious thing to do in terms of time (ample) and equipment (minimal). Moreover it was an artistic enterprise for which, unlike playing Mozart's *Requiem* or dancing *Swan Lake*, I believed myself to be qualified by nearly two decades of reading. After all, that was the only training most of my favourite writers had undergone. "Read good authors with passionate attention," runs Robert Louis Stevenson's advice to a young writer; "refrain altogether from reading bad ones."

In campsites and cheap hotels I did my best to imitate Trollope, writing for so many hours a day. I wrote in pencil, rubbing out frequently, on every other line of the right-hand pages of a spiral notebook. I filled one notebook, began another, filled that, too. My novel was growing, but when, near the end of the year, I reread the notebooks, something curious occurred. Whenever I read, say, the opening of *Great Expectations,* sentences and paragraphs vanished; I was on the marsh with Pip and the fearsome convict. But my own prose left me obstinately earthbound: Once again the words were only marks on the page, rather than a window into another world. I tried to tell myself that this strange stodginess was the burden of authorship: words, which could transport others were mute to their maker. Years later in America I overheard a poet saying, I claim to like all my poems equally, but I can tell what I really think by seeing which ones I send to *The New Yorker.*

One respect in which I followed Stevenson's advice that year was by reading E.M. Forster. The Penguin paperbacks of his novels were widely available in Western Europe and North Africa. Amongst secondhand books there was almost invariably a copy of *Howard's End* or *Room With a View.* After my neo-Victorian childhood these novels were the opposite of mute; they resonated as loudly as and much longer than Adela Quested's echo in the Marabar Caves. How well Forster understood that embarrassment is a major emotion, that we are all governed by the opinions of others and by the great triumvirate of class, race, and money. Of course I believed myself, sitting in the gardens of the Alhambra, exploring the Casbah of Tangiers, to be a successful fugitive from such bourgeois notions, but what a pleasure it was to look back. "Only connect," I murmured.

What did this have to do with my novel? Unfortunately not much. I had no idea, not an inkling, how Forster put his seamless, glittering, playful books together. The notion of dismantling a novel, examining the point of view or the transitions, was still entirely foreign. On a recent transatlantic flight I reread *A Passage to India;* it's easy to see now why I was baffled on first reading.

The novel is so tenacious in its intelligence, so deft in its handling of point of view, and the voice, the glorious voice, rises over everything, controlling every fan and slipper and semicolon. The part I had remembered, Adela's visit to the caves and her subsequent accusation of Doctor Aziz, turns out to be the centre of the book but not, in some odd way, the climax. The third section of the novel, "Temple," which takes place two years later during the Hindu birth ceremony, shows us that Forster is pursuing something altogether larger, more ineffable, than the fuss about Adela.

My own novel was called, prophetically, *The Oubliette*, after the French dungeon where prisoners were left to languish until they were forgotten. The one small shard of defence I can offer is that it was not autobiographical but was based on a school friend and her mother, both of whom had embarked upon ardent affairs. (To understand why this should strike me as original material you have to know that I grew up in a world where the word "divorce" was never uttered except in connection with Edward VIII and Mrs. Simpson.) In real life, happily, these women prospered. My friend studied music and went on to become an Alexander Method teacher; her mother made a happy second marriage, and so, following a brief period of dishevelment, did her father. In my novel, however, the mother gives up her lover after his wife commits suicide. (While reading Forster, I had also read Gide's *Strait Is the Gate* with its mysterious acts of renunciation.) I don't recall what fate I bestowed on the daughter. I keep the manuscript on the lowest shelf of my bookcase in America, but a semiserious illness (and an utter dearth of alternatives) would be needed to make me open the dusty box and reread those pages.

The problems with *The Oubliette* are too numerous to mention, but amongst them are certainly the following: I had no idea how to create the illusion of dialogue, no sense of pacing, no thought for what sort of unit a chapter could or should be, no understanding of the purpose of description in narrative, and perhaps strangest of all, no notion of the crucial role suspense plays in fiction, especially longer fiction. As a reader I had enjoyed the fruits of these skills in other writers without the least comprehension of how they were achieved. I had spent many happy hours in the house of fiction, but I knew nothing about plumbing or wiring or putting up drywall.

Perhaps more seriously, I had failed to grasp the truth of the Anglo-Irish writer Elizabeth Bowen's remark: The greatest sin in a novel is irrelevance. One thing I knew for sure about novels was that they went on for a while, so I dutifully threw in a mass of detail. I described the toast, the trees, the birds, the curtains. This, I thought, was what the project of realism was all about. Putting aside that misunderstanding, how could I have comprehended the deeply complicated question of relevance when, even after months of work, I couldn't explain what truly interested me in the material. (I'm echoing here W.H. Auden's dazzlingly simple advice: Write about what interests you.) I wanted to write a novel, not necessarily this one.

I did find an agent for *The Oubliette*, and he sent it around, and various people sent it back with the usual kind remarks. Meanwhile I had turned to stories. My year of travel was over and these fitted better with the split shifts I was working as a waitress in Toronto. I would write in the morning before going off to serve lunch to harried office workers and again in the afternoon before the more enviable dinner crowd showed up. I still read omnivorously, but the connection between reading and writing remained as mysterious as ever.

A turning point in my snail's progress came when the Irish Canadian novelist Brian Moore spent a term at the University of Toronto as writer in residence. The secretary who made his appointments didn't press me about my credentials, and I turned up in my waitress' black skirt and white blouse, nervously clutching a story. What Mr. Moore did then was astonishing. From the breast pocket of his tweed jacket, he produced a fountain pen and, pen in hand, read the story aloud, imitating all the characters, even the pigs; the story was set on a farm near where I had grown up. "Now would she say that?" he pondered. "Or should there be a little more about the ponies, that nickering sound they make?"

I brought him that same story on half a dozen occasions, and each time he read it aloud. No detail was too small for his attention. He showed me that those marks on the page, which since my early struggles with "Percy" I had ceased to apprehend individually, could make all the difference. He showed me that a good sentence speaks even to its maker and that we can learn to recognise our own mediocrity. Now, after years of teaching, I admire both his kindness and his acumen in not allowing me to leave a single sheet of paper on his desk.

So I asked people how they wanted their steak and whether they cared for dessert and I continued to write. At the age of thirty I knew no one else who wrote fiction or even aspired to do so, but one by one the stories crept into print. When at last I returned to the novel, it was through the narrow gate of story-writing. In a British newspaper I read a letter by a woman about her daughter. Nine-year-old Louise dominated the family with her fierce temper and fanatical sense of order. She complained if a chair was moved so much as an inch or if her father arrived home five minutes late. Holidays were out of the question, as indeed was any change of routine. Her brothers, both older, dreaded to cross her. And Louise herself was immune to punishment. I still recall the heart-breaking conclusion, the writer's hopelessness as she watched her husband prepare to leave her, her sons grow increasingly aloof. If my spouse behaved like this, she wrote, I could divorce him, but how can I divorce my daughter?

This letter resonated for me at a number of levels. As a terrifically well-behaved stepchild, I had seen my father honor my stepmother's every whim. Then, in my early twenties, I had myself become an absent-minded stepmother, struggling with the other side of the equation. So I was keenly interested in what occurs when romantic and familial love collide. Over several months I tried to fit this idea—a child who ignores the social contract—into twenty pages, twenty-five maximum. Eventually, reluctantly, I was forced to accept that the topic required the space of a novel.

By this time I had moved, in one of those odd aberrations of North American life, from waitressing to teaching. Most of my students were working, as I had been for a number of years, on short stories. Perhaps no surprise then that my editor's first comment on an early draft of *Homework* was that I had written a story-writer's novel. Every chapter ended with an epiphany. Close the book, dear reader, I might as well have said. Working on stories had taught me much about scene and sentence but not that eloquent balancing of the long and short lines of suspense that a novel requires.

II

The Fat Novel

Thinking about Forster in general and *A Passage to India* in particular took me back to Henry James, who is surely Forster's most immediate ancestor in terms of subject matter and, to some extent, technique. James' Americans go to Europe. Forster's English men and women go to Italy, or India. Both authors were sharply aware of the fictional possibilities of leaving home and / or the stranger coming to town (according to John Gardner, the two great plots), and both used these plots to explore not only issues of culture, class, and race but also the erotic and spiritual lives of their protagonists.

I had read *The Portrait of a Lady* at university, James being among the safely dead, but going back to it, as a writer, was a revelation, not least because of the amazing fact that it was written as a serial. In 1876, the year he published *Roderick Hudson,* James settled in London. The years immediately following find him referring in

both notebooks and letters to his new, big novel. When William
James pronounced *The Europeans* thin, Henry wrote back, "I don't
at all despair of doing something fat." In a letter to his mother he
described the new novel as being to his previous work like wine to
water. But first he had to create some breathing space. He cashed
in on the success of *Daisy Miller* by the rapid production and publication of three shorter works: *The Europeans, Washington Square,*
and *Confidence.* All of this put James in a position to negotiate what
for most of us would be the opposite of breathing space. He
arranged simultaneous serialisation of the unwritten novel in *The
Atlantic* in America and *MacMillans* in Britain, originally promising
between six and eight monthly episodes and finally producing
fourteen. He began work in the spring of 1880; the first episode
was published that autumn.

Rereading the opening of *Portrait* I was struck by how firmly
James gives his instructions to the reader and by the odd uncertainties of tone in the description of the three men having tea on
the lawn of an English country-house beside the Thames, waiting
for the arrival of Mrs. Touchett and her mysterious niece. Out
onto that gilded lawn, into that glorious company, sails Isabel
Archer, the young woman of no obvious talents whom James tells
us only one man in twenty will have the discrimination to appreciate and with whom everyone in the novel, save her husband, falls
in love.

Beginning with the title, James never loses sight of the large question—what will Isabel Archer do? what will become of her?—that is
the long line of suspense that governs the novel from first to last. And
within the scope of that long line he poses many smaller questions,
which, like the arches of a viaduct, carry us from chapter to chapter—who is Madame Merle? will Henrietta Stackpole alienate everyone? will Posie marry her heart's desire? will Isabel ever discover that
Ralph is responsible for her fortune? will Caspar Goodwood ever give
up? As one question is answered, another opens up, leading us
onward, ever onward.

James was vitally aware of the need to earn what he calls the writer's living wage: the reader's attention. In the preface to the revised edition of *Portrait*, written with nearly thirty years of hindsight, he muses on the danger of having too little story and claims to have taken every possible provision for the reader's amusement. Certainly W.D. Howells, James' editor at *The Atlantic*, was less than impressed by the entertainment value of the early episodes. After the first couple he wrote to complain that Isabel was overanalysed and that there was too much of Henrietta. And James' sister Alice—clearly the family believed in vigorous criticism—pondered whether Isabel would ever befriend someone like Henrietta. James agreed with Howells and defended himself against Alice.

In the preface he remarks, "It is a familiar truth to the novelist, at the strenuous hour, that, as certain elements in any work are of the essence, so others are only of the form." Some characters, he continues, belong to the subject directly, others but indirectly. Henrietta Stackpole is an example of the latter. James compares her first to one of the wheels of the coach where "the subject alone is ensconced, in the form of its 'hero and heroine.'" Then, shifting the metaphor, comments that Henrietta may run beside the coach for all she's worth, may cling to it until she's out of breath, but that she never so much as gets her foot on the step. Isabel, James reminds us repeatedly, is a heroine in the Shakespearean sense.

It's interesting to look at these comments in the light of Lionel Trilling's famous critique of *A Passage to India*. "The characters," Trilling says, "are in the events, the events are not in them: we want a larger Englishman than Fielding, a weightier Indian than Aziz." Forster, he concludes, is writing a political novel of an unusual kind, one in which "the characters are of sufficient size for the plot; they are not large enough for the story—and that indeed is the point of the story."

Part of what Trilling is pointing to here, if I understand him correctly, is one of the great virtues of *A Passage to India*: Forster's determination not to have a hero or heroine. No one is riding in his coach; everyone is clinging to the wheels as it careens along.

This lack of a hero, of an obvious centre of empathy, leads to an even more subtle balancing of the long and short lines of suspense, a subtlety that must have been particularly acute for Forster's original readers, many of whom would have known the formulaic Indian romances that were popular at that time. I have to confess that on first reading *A Passage to India* I had no idea what the large question was—the long line of suspense—but read happily from one small question to the next. Would the Bridge party work out? would Adela accept Ronnie? would Aziz and Fielding succeed in becoming friends? would Adela recant? When the last veil finally fell, in the triumphant third section, "Temple," and Forster showed his hand, I gasped with recognition and delight. Of course, this had been here all along, since the moonlit night when Aziz meets Mrs. Moore in the mosque, but reading as I was in the Jamesian tradition, looking for someone to ride in the coach with, I had failed to notice these other possibilities.

In my novel *Homework* I did have a long line of suspense—how would the battle end between the narrator and her stepdaughter?—but as my decisive chapter endings showed, I had no notion of how to manage the shorter lines of suspense or even, indeed, that they were necessary.

In other respects, too, *Homework* was the work of a story-writer. Although I knew enough to set the novel in a city I loved, Edinburgh, and to give the characters jobs I was familiar with, I did not yet fully realise the importance of what might crudely be called stuff in a novel: the peculiar circumstances that render the characters vivid and interesting. In a short story you can get away without much stuff, a sentence or two about breeding Labradors or stripping wallpaper, but in a novel, or at least most novels, it is essential; perhaps never more so than when the plot is basically domestic. James, it could be argued, is not a good model in this respect. Even at his best he is short on stuff; Henrietta clearly represents some gesture towards filling that gap, as do his exquisite descriptions of houses. Then of course both he and Forster use travel as stuff.

What embarrasses me most about *Homework,* I mean not the book itself but how I worked on it, was my absolute belief in my editor. My days among the classics of the nineteenth and early twentieth centuries, combined with my own early rejections, had left me with the impression that publication was a sure sign of perfection. I don't mean that I entertained this idea at the rational level. By this time I was letting Stevenson down on a regular basis, reading contemporary fiction. Publication, I had discovered, was conferred on a surprising number of less-than-perfect books, ranging from the mildly flawed to the utterly mediocre, and all of these books had editors. In spite of so much contrary evidence, however, I believed my editor to be infallible. As long as she didn't point out a problem, everything was fine. I forgot the message of Brian Moore and his fountain pen. No need for me, the mere author, to worry that the account of making dinner or making love was tedious; look, the margins were empty.

III

The Problem of Evil

Besides their material and their sense of character, James and Forster share one other major writerly strength; both were keen observers of the world around them and both knew how to transform their observations into art. Over and over in James' notebooks, we see the raw material of his fiction—the gesture, the glance, the phrase—captured and brooded upon. Dinner parties, as Leon Edel so felicitously remarks, were his laboratory. Forster has the same acute gift for noticing what he needs for his work. Paradoxically one of the many things I needed to learn from reading books was how to read the world.

One snowy evening, walking by Boston Common on my way to teach a class of graduate students, I saw a group of protesters from Operation Rescue standing beside a bus shelter. The two images—the lurid posters and the illuminated shelter—fused in my mind, and by the time I reached the classroom I had decided to write a novel about someone who finds a baby in a bus station. Who should that finder be? At first I thought a version of myself. Then I knew it had to be a man, a man in a suit. I recalled an article I had read about insider trading and how this relatively new crime was affecting bankers and financiers. So my novel *Criminals* began to come together, and this time I determined, for good or ill, to use what I had learned in my reading: to write something I would (at least hypothetically) enjoy reading, to assume that reading my own work was no different from reading other people's. If I was bored by a sentence, a paragraph, a chapter, everyone else would be too.

I had a plot, I had a subplot, I had stuff. I clung to Elizabeth Bowen's remark and interpreted it as meaning, at least at one level, cut ruthlessly. I happily paid homage to some of my favorite Victorians and included a novel within the novel, which I in turn defended by including a bad review. I understood at last Graham Greene's comment that the hardest task facing the novelist is how to pass time, and made the events occur in a little over a week. I recognised that whatever my editor's talents I remained the author and read every chapter aloud.

All this ruthlessness paid off in creating a readable manuscript. Still, something mysterious, ineffable was needed. I had the plot, but the deeper level of meaning—what the plot was intended to reveal—remained murky, inchoate.

When Forster visited India for the first time in 1912, he was thirty-three and had written and published four novels without much trouble. He began *A Passage to India* after his return to England in 1913 and managed to write eight chapters before setting the pages aside in favor of *Maurice,* his only openly homosexual and posthumously published novel. December 31st, 1914, finds him announcing in his diary, "Shall never complete another novel." In the face of the First World War fiction struck him as increasingly futile.

Forster spent most of the war in Egypt, working for the Red Cross in Alexandria. During those years he produced a slew of pamphlets and critical works but no fiction. A second visit to India in 1921 only made him despair further of his chapters: "As soon as they were confronted with the country they purported to describe, they seemed to wilt and go dead and I could do nothing with them." But back in England, urged on by Leonard Woolf, he returned to those wilted pages. Finally, on January 21st, 1924, he declared the novel finished. Life being different then, it was published a few months later, in early June, and became a huge success.

No one would want to suffer Forster's difficulties and despairs, but surely everyone would want to write a novel as sublime as the one that resulted. Reading *A Passage to India* gives no clue to its tattered history, the fits and starts in which it was composed, the uncertainties that Forster suffered throughout and especially in writing the scenes set at the Marabar Caves. The novel was indubitably changed by the events of the intervening years. The war, living in Alexandria, and the Amritsar Massacre of 1919 had a profound effect on Forster's views of colonisation and civilisation. At a different level his reading of Proust was immensely influential.

It's illuminating to compare one of the many early drafts of the cave scene with the final version. In 1913 Forster wrote: "She struck out and he got hold of her other hand and forced her against the wall, he got both her hands in one of his, and then felt at her breasts. 'Mrs. Moore,' she yelled. 'Ronny—don't let him, save me.'" In the published version of the scene, written almost a decade later, Adela and Aziz approach the caves. Adela, preoccupied with thoughts of her forthcoming marriage, asks Aziz whether he is married and then, "in her honest, decent, inquisitive way," how many wives he has. "One, one in my own particular case," sputters Aziz, and plunges into one of the several caves. Adela, "quite unconscious that she had said the wrong thing, and not seeing him," also goes into a cave. There the chapter ends. We never learn what really did happen in the cave, only what didn't. The author himself, later in life, always claimed not to know.

Forster's decade of gestation was a time not only of widespread political upheaval but also of huge private changes. Living in Alexandria, he became friends with the poet Cavafy, who unlike Forster was openly homosexual. By both precept and example Cavafy seems to have encouraged the shy Englishman to new boldness. In October 1916 Forster wrote to his friend Florence Berger, "Yesterday for the first time in my life I parted with respectability." He excised the words "in my life" and then added "I have felt the step would be taken for many months. I have tried it before. It has left me curiously sad." He was thirty-eight years old.

Later he admitted to some hyperbole. On October 3rd, 1917, he wrote again to Florence: "R. has been parted with, and in the simplest most inevitable way, just as you hoped. I am so happy— not for the actual pleasure but because the last barrier has fallen."

It's tempting to speculate, with Forster's encouragement, that the falling of that final barrier contributed to the rewriting of the cave scene, the stripping away of physical detail, and to his eloquent rendition of Godpole's view of the situation. "I ask you," Fielding says to Godpole, "did he [Aziz] do it or not? Is that plain?" Godpole replies:

"I am informed that an evil action was performed in the Marabar Hills, and that a highly esteemed English lady is now seriously ill in consequence. My answer to that is this: that action was performed by Dr. Aziz." He stopped and sucked in his thin cheeks. "It was performed by the guide." He stopped again. "It was performed by you." Now he had an air of daring and coyness. "It was performed by me." He looked shyly down the sleeve of his own coat. "And by my students. It was even performed by the lady herself. When evil occurs, it expresses the whole of the universe. Similarly when good occurs."

Finally Forster, like James, is after the age-old moral questions. When Isabel at last learns the truth about Madame Merle she wonders whether perhaps now she has encountered a phenomenon known previously only from the Bible: wickedness.

Forster lived forty-five years after the publication of *A Passage to India*. He wrote essays, stories, criticism, but no more novels. To those who asked why not he gave various answers. To one he claimed he was bored by the fictional convention of keeping to the point of view of a single character. To another that "the upheavals in society and psychology and physics (all at the same time) are too much for a form of art which assumed a certain amount of stability in all three." To Siegfried Sassoon he remarked, "I shall never write another novel—my patience with ordinary people has given out." Perhaps too the discovery of a romantic happiness that could not, by Forster's lights, be portrayed in fiction helped to turn him away from the novel.

IV

Krishna

In the case of *Criminals* I found, I hope I found, the deeper level of meaning by looking more closely at what I had written, by coming to understand, sentence by sentence, what was truly relevant to my concerns. All along I had been moving towards a reenactment of the judgment of Solomon when the two "mothers" struggled over the baby. I had seen their struggle as being fatal.

Now I realised that I was not writing a tragic novel. The baby I had killed in my original last chapter was revived and everyone lived unhappily ever after, which was, after all, something I knew much more about than murder and mayhem.

Stevenson's advice to the young writer is misleadingly simple, a Zen koan in disguise. Read everything that is good, nothing that is bad. And then what? Perhaps if he had written at more length he might helpfully have expanded on his imperatives. Read everything that is good for the good of your soul. Then, learn to read as a writer, to search out that hidden machinery, which it is the business of art to conceal and the business of the apprentice to comprehend. Read work that is less than good, work in progress, to see that machinery more clearly. Learn to read your own work as if it were that of another. Admit your own judgments. We know our own strengths and weaknesses, even when we strive not to.

And then, then you have to hope for grace or luck, the Lares and Penates of fiction, to knock at your door. The kind of luck that brought Forster on his second visit to India to the nine-day festival commemorating the birth of Krishna and that gave him the gorgeous third section of *A Passage to India*. Few writers get steadily better, but many get unsteadily so.

GEOFFREY WOLFF

Communal Solitude

Let's stipulate: of writers' programs, workshops, conferences, festivals, symposia, colloquies, leagues, guilds, readings, and jamborees there is no dearth. Like many a writer of my acquaintance, I have worked with student fictioneers during the school year and camped lakeside or mountainside or pasture-side or seaside at writers' conferences during summer weeks. Flathead Lake, Aspen, Squaw Valley, the Land of the Midnight Sun, western North Carolina, Vermont ... It was in Vermont, in a pretty barn, that an evening speaker attempted to summarize for the gathered would-bes the writer's situation; he told a tale of a New York poet who received in the mail from a travel agent a congratulatory notice that he had won a no-strings-attached all-expenses-paid cruise to Jamaica. He wasn't born yesterday, this poet, so he tossed the coupon in the trash, together with all those crumpled pages of the sestina that kept coming out a stanza short. The travel agent phoned:

"Well," he asked, "did you get the good news?"

The poet admitted that the mail had been delivered, but he was no fool. "What's the catch?"

"No catch. I've got your ticket right here on my desk, waiting for a pickup."

"Why me?"

"You're a writer, no?"

"I am."

"There you go. This is for writers only, a special thing, recognition."

So the poet fetched his ticket from the travel agent, and the following morning embarked from a Hudson River pier on his winter cruise to the Caribbean. He had an obstructed view of the rough sea from his assigned seat below decks. He recognized many fellow creative writers, but they were all too busy rowing to pass the time of day. A burly peg-leg with an eye-patch beat on a bass drum with one hand and with the other rhythmically whipped the artists' backs with a rawhide lash. After a couple of weeks of this agonizing passage, the toilers were commanded to ship their oars and rest, and to regard from the slits that served as portholes yonder coconut-palmed isle and talcy pink beach. The vessel rolled beam to the surf half a mile offshore. The sightseers gazed longingly, and presently came the incessant drumbeat, and the lash, and the stroke quickened and they labored north toward home. Finally they passed Sandy Hook, and espied Lady Liberty, and nosed up the Hudson. The poet turned to his seat-mate:

"Do we tip the drummer?"

"I didn't last time."

That night at Bread Loaf was not the first time I had heard a writer recount in a public place this allegory, and it wouldn't be the last. Repetition, after all, is one of narrative's boss devices. Reiteration was caretaker to Homer's epics, the wellspring of the wisdom of the tribe, but it is also the reflexive offload of conventional wisdom, of cliché. And the ruling cliché at every summer writers' conference I have ever attended is that the chosen are an elect crew who have overcome daunting statistical odds to be invited to pay to enlist, and that the crew to which they have been admitted must be as brave as warriors to carry the banner of art in the crusade against the uninitiated. The message is often bewildering: Welcome to our band, brothers and sisters; after the hazing ends, the real humiliation begins. The seniors emphasize to the frosh that nothing but hard times lie ahead: measly advances, editors slipshod or roughshod, publicists who are the envy of the Witness Protection Program. And should word of a book slip out, reviewers—assassins as bored in their blood thirst as sharks—know what to do ... What have I missed? Distracted readers, impatient booksellers ... welcome!

The fee-payers, whatever they are called, sit wearing thin smiles, scribbling the free-galley-vacation cautionary tale into notebooks, nodding sagely, looking up at the podium, itching to cross the gangplank. There is an exacerbated sense of hierarchy encouraged by many of these summer writing camps, and I begin with Bread Loaf because it is among such gatherings the most venerable (Robert Frost, who titled such summering "barding around," was an early but not the earliest Bread Loafer) and probably most venerated, and when I taught there (mid-Seventies to mid-Eighties) it was surely the most scaled and subordinated.

The Great Chain of Being that was Bread Loaf descended in links from the summit of Staff to the trough of Auditor. We Staff were personages who had had three or more books published. We were paid what we were paid, and endowed with comfortable dwellings to which we could bring our families. We ate communally, on the house, waited on by Waiters and Waitresses, who were positioned below Staff Assistants (two books, and paid less than Staff to do Staff work), below Fellows (at least one published book, and paid less than Staff Assistants), below Scholars (story or poetry [that would be poem*s*, not *a* poem] published in Nationally Recognized Magazine, a free ride but no payday), but above Contributors (who rendered full fees to have their work judged by Faculty, Staff Assistants, or Fellows), and way above Auditors (who were obliged to check their pencils and paper at the door, and who remitted full freight to observe the some-times noble and sometimes comic operatic proceedings).

Once upon a time, before my time, Staff sat themselves at din-ner on a dais, a plywood platform from which the drunkards among them would sometimes tumble after a long twilight of highballs at Treman. Treman was Bread Loaf's House of Lords, as in drunk as. (It was on the pretty mowed meadow outside Treman, during a cocktail hour in the late summer of the early Eighties, that an airplane swooped low over the assembled writers and dumped scandal, in the form of leaflets marked WANTED! "For Fraud, Falsehood, Violation of Court Orders, Passing Bad Checks, etc., etc., *John Gardner*, author of such frauds as *On Moral Fiction*.") Hijinks at Treman were reserved for Staff (the late Gardner, for instance, whose first wife was cross enough with him about alimony and more personal disputes to have hired Sky Writers, Ltd.), and to Staff Assistants, Fellows, Administrators, and Guests. Waitpersons, for instance, were left to arrange ad hoc drinking parties for themselves 'neath elm and maple, where guitars were played and pairings arranged. They had the fun.

Youth has its advantages, and fun is among them. Not among them is professional serenity, and an institution like Bread Loaf— and there are many institutions that aspire to be like Bread Loaf—seems to have been designed to translate the apprentice's natural career anxiety into wild temperamental chaos. One year in the late Seventies a Bread Loaf Guest, assistant poetry editor at a much esteemed Nationally Recognized Journal, ran a casting couch enterprise among the prettiest poets of the many pretty female Waitpersons. Worse, these cute poets were obliged to provide the couch, inasmuch as the editor didn't wish to intrude upon his wife, napping in their gratis cottage. This editor, who wore a Eustace Tilley tee shirt in case anyone doubted his bona fides, would have himself invited to the aspiring poet's quarters, where lovey-dovey would precede a study of the poet's portfolio, followed by a judgment of the verses' utility to the majestic periodical. After love came candor. The poems were judged to be without consequence, ambition, voice, reach, gravitas, hope. A lecture would be provided, during the recumbent cigarette smoking: Poetry matters ... is a sacred trust, etcetera. As word of the truth-telling gallant's work rose osmotically toward the Staff and seeped downhill even unto Auditors, word also spread of awful insults to the swain's food back in the kitchen. Always treat the little people well, especially if they're in the food service industry, or if they're writers.

When I look back at Bread Loaf from a distance of thirteen years, I can't imagine why everyone there didn't go nuts. Many did, of course. The mix—of ex-lovers, agents, editors, prize-winners, prize-losers, prize-givers, prize-takers-away, or Auditors who had hoped to be Contributors—was toxic. Envy was epidemic. Way back when, Archibald MacLeish had given a poetry reading at Bread Loaf. He was interrupted in this journey not by woods on a snowy evening but by Robert Frost creating a disruption, setting a fire on that August night so that he could noisily stamp out the smoky conflagration. And what papers were put ablaze? Not an Auditor's, of course, but perhaps a Contributor's?

Readings were blood-sport competitions. We gathered in that bucolic place casually got up in sweaters and flannel shirts, blue jeans and hiking shorts. But the auditorium was as consequential as a courtroom, and the outcomes as just. After the readings—around the piano in the barn, or at the Treman bar, or on a blanket in the meadow—there were dissections, and these were frequently unmerciful, and sometimes parodic. But when I look back on those crisp August weeks in Vermont's Middlebury Gap I remember best not the cruelty, nor office-party license, nor the log-rolling, nor the blind staggers boozing, nor the nutcases carried away year after year in police cars or ambulances. I remember those public lectures and readings, some of them life-changingly audacious, serious and exposed. Tim O'Brien's *Going After Cacciato*, for instance, and John Irving's *The World According to Garp*, and Toni Morrison's *Song of Solomon*, and Stanley Elkin's extraordinary triptych of long stories, *The Living End*, each—"The Conventional Wisdom," "The Bottom Line," "The State of the Art"—written during successive summers so that he'd have something to read at Bread Loaf.

No, it was more complicated than that. Everything is always more complicated than it seems, and what's especially more complicated than the conventional wisdom suggests is the value of institutionalized teaching and study of writing. Irony is imported from city and campus to the hinterlands where creative hootenannies are organized. Cynics are thick on the Arcadian and picturesque ground. The fissure between writers' plummy discourse and their tosspot goats-and-monkeys summer play-penning is irresistible to exposé journalists sent undercover to plump up the Sunday arts and leisure sections at autumn's dawn. Fish in a barrel, really, lifting the rolled log to reveal underneath sexual shenanigans, nonsensical dicta. Even more ubiquitous are gratuitous swipes at graduate writing programs, at what is casually diminished as Workshop Fiction (to be distinguished from *New Yorker* Fiction, whatever it may have been). Whenever the putatively sorry state of the arts today is invoked, a few corrupting influences are reflexively invoked: Minimalism (or Southern Gothic excess), or Kmart realism, or—for sorry shame!—the memoir, and eternally, the baneful influence of creative writing courses, particularly at the graduate school level.

The inventory of workshop vices is invoked by now routinely in the better Sunday supplements and in *Harper's*:

~ The spurious professionalization (it's handy to use that ugly locution)—by way of what academies term "the terminal degree"—of fictional art. This is seen in elevated creative circles as a threat to the miraculous genius of the sublime, much as the social sciences' graphs and statistics are seen to be a sad burlesque of the scientific method. Apprentice to the workshop or to the muse, one guild or another, choose your poison: the union that shuts out MFA recipients for their voc-school training, or the union that shuts out the unterminally degreed.

~ The MFA process is renounced as a kind of pyramid scheme, whereby writers in possession of the franchise, well-paid to teach at a dozen or so "top" programs, seed an unending harvest of certified writers clamoring for sub-franchises at newly created MFA programs elsewhere. (Don't scoff: There are hundreds of programs.)

~ In such a Gresham's Law-ruled land, the appetite for fee-payers produces more writers than readers, seducing a permanent cultural underclass of embittered would-bes humbugged into indebting themselves with ruinous students loans on the fat chance that the Prize Patrol will arrive at their doorsteps with a contract from Farrar, Straus.

~ Some MFA programs grant degrees to—certify, that is—as many as twenty fiction writers per year. There haven't been twenty American fiction writers worthy of the name since the beginning of the Cold War, and the rise of the MFA program.

~ It's a staple of interviews with mandarin creative writers—rarely poets—that employment by the academy is corrupt. The writers who view their lessers through such an unforgiving lens are most frequently commercially successful, and very often the beneficiaries of Hollywood's fecund benefits. Those who can't, teach; those who can, sell to Dreamworks and Disney. It's always risky to accuse others of selling out. As Tom McGuane has wonderfully observed, the very artistes who revere Saint Jean Genet for his thieving and Jack Abbott for his (pre-parole) violence are quick to deplore as polluted by misemployment a novelist selling out to (as opposed to honorably stealing from or slaying) a movie producer.

Poets have always barded around. I heard Frost read at my high school (and MacLeish too). Robert Lowell taught at Harvard with Elizabeth Bishop and at Boston University (where he made an impression on Sylvia Plath and Anne Sexton); Theodore Roethke served time at the University of Washington; John Berryman at Minnesota; even Delmore Schwartz got gigs, at Syracuse, and before that at Princeton, where I had the luck to have R[ichard] P. Blackmur as a creative writing advisor. And boy oh boy, did he give me advice! But after I flagellate myself with the advice he gave—which was to bury my novel (*Certain Half-Deserted Streets*, like the titles of all undergraduate novels of the time lifted from a T.S. Eliot line) in a desk drawer, lock the desk drawer, throw away the key, and set fire to the desk—let me say how uncomfortable was everyone concerned in those palmy days with the locution "creative writing." It sounded silly and shammy—like that apocryphal (Jesus, I hope!) course in basket-weaving at Rollins—and at the same time spuriously puffed up, in the lingo of the day, phony, pseudo.

It helped that the great poets and novelists of the Fifties and Sixties who taught creative writing weren't themselves institutional creatures. As learned and brilliant as Blackmur was, he hadn't bothered with a high school diploma, let alone college study. To be taught creative writing by Blackmur was as unlike being "workshopped" as a learning experience can be. A legendary close reader, perhaps the purest of the New Critics, his reading of *Certain Half-Deserted Streets*, and certain half-assed Geoffrey Wolff poems and stories, was arm's-length and then some. But sometimes he'd fall, like a hawk on a mouse, upon some felicity of expression, some agreeable sequence of syllables or surprise of syntax: "There!" he'd say. "That's how to do it." My failures didn't interest him, in two ways. They *really* didn't interest him, as in they bored him, and they didn't dumbfound him any more than Dr. Johnson would have been amazed to see a dog walk clumsily on its hind legs.

In my time, no writer I knew aspired to apply to a graduate school of writing. Iowa was already an esteemed institution, and writers as fine as Flannery O'Connor had studied there, but it wasn't on our radar screens. At Princeton, then, creative writing was taught one-on-one, student alone in a room for an hour or so every week with Blackmur or Julian Moynahan or Kingsley Amis. In Blackmur's case, if it was after lunch when we met, he'd be what I thought then was distracted and know now was drunk. He might read his mail, aloud. It was interesting mail, familiar and irreverent and what seemed then (and maybe was) stunningly witty correspondence from fellow writers about fellow writers, and—more crucially— about writing. Blackmur read these letters aloud to some of his students because it was easier in the afternoon to quote than to think. The impression on us cannot be overstated. As a magician's apprentices we were being admitted to the place offstage where the miracles are fabricated. We had the illusion—with apprentices it is almost always an illusion and almost always a necessary illusion—that we had been admitted.

Now, of course, admission means something else: an application form, statement of purpose, autobiographical summary, perhaps GREs, a transcript, letters of commendation, and—not at all incidentally—a portfolio of representative work. Admission now, for all its system of checks and balances, seems to me more exclusive than it was when I thought of myself as an apprentice. There's more up-or-out to it, a conviction that evolution is marked by advancement in rank, with material compensation expected for each hurdle jumped. Admission for such secular old-timers as myself was somehow self-determined: we didn't think of ourselves as writers—I speak for myself here—until we had published as writers. We thought of ourselves rather as devotees, and our stations of the cross were internally marked by what we accepted as private convictions. I would never have dreamed of asking R.P. Blackmur what a gifted Princeton sophomore asked me: Can you guarantee that if I read and write and revise for—how many years again?—I'll make a good living as a writer?

This begs the question: what does *gifted* mean? Imaginative? Not necessarily: This inflates the value of novelty. Persistent? So are long-haul truckers (whose occupation novel-writing in many ways resembles). Self-certainty? Arrogance—demanding too much of the reader—can be a curse exceeded only by humility, expecting too little of oneself. Music is necessary, and while no one would argue that everyone learns music as easily as everyone else, likewise no one would sensibly propose that musical training, guided practice, is unavailing.

Why then do so many writers profess that writing cannot be taught? Probably because no writer can be conditioned by a workshop to write well, only to write better. Knowing what I know about the feral competition among young would-be writers to gain admission to the better graduate writing programs, and having burned into shame's maddeningly reliable memory-bank the sentences and sequences of *Certain Half-Deserted Streets*, I'm more than a little certain that I wouldn't cut the mustard were I trying then to join the writing program where I teach now. I also believe that we'd be wrong to turn me away, but I know that we're wrong to turn many people away. My work was purply and over layered with gilt and ripe with pretense. I felt an authentic need to make sentences, but the sentences I made were unfelt. I was, that is, learning. I might have learned more quickly in a writing program, or the workshop might have driven me away from the calling prematurely. God knows it can be a brutalizing experience.

As an apprentice workshop teacher I once had the awful brainstorm that I'd let my students workshop—"woodshed" was more like it—my novel in progress. The experience—especially the tender and manifestly unenthusiastic good manners of the undergraduates—was mortifying, and it was chastening. I don't ever want to have it done to me again, but I believe in doing it to those who want it done. I believe in the virtue of a workshop as a sanctuary, a place where nothing matters but words in sequence and the stories achieved by words in sequence.

Whoever pretended that a gift can be taught? But isn't it a peculiarly know-nothing faith in the irrational to celebrate the sentimental agnosticism that holds that words are undiscussable? Would any writer seriously hold that to teach or study reading is to perpetuate a fraud on art? I understand—I hope—the writer's hostility toward institutions, but I really don't understand the punch of anti-workshop belligerence, unless it is a repudiation of the very notion of community. This, unlike most vices of artistic religion, doesn't have its roots in Romanticism, but rather in Hemingway's Nick Adams, alone on the Big Two-Hearted River, reliant on self-monitored skills and decorums, which someone—by the way—taught him.

In my day it was thought to be unseemly to be present for the sharing in a public place of what one had wrought in private. Musicians, counted by writers as kin, have never enjoyed the luxury of such an odd scruple. But many writers still feel suspicion for those of their fellows who enjoy performing, reading aloud to audiences, and I have a hunch that this suspicion is symptomatic of the odd process—unteachable indeed!—that turns a disease of sneakiness into a wholesome expression of sensibility: writers like to throw the message across their neighbor's fence, and run like hell. In the safety of fellow writers' company, novelists will tell the horror story of sitting in a room watching her husband read deadpan her meant-to-be-hilarious first draft, or of sitting across an airplane aisle from a reader who glances distractedly for a few moments at her just-published book before dog-earing it on page seven and turning to the in-flight magazine crossword puzzle.

In my day strict lessons were meant to be taken from such humiliations. Well, to hell with my day. Believe me, there's solitude aplenty out there, and whatever illusion of community can be created by the honorable fabrication of a workshop, well, that's fine by me.

DEBORAH EISENBERG

Resistance

You'll have noticed, I expect, that when asked why they write, a number of writers, fiction writers at least, answer that it's because they can't do anything else. I am among this number, and I say it—"because I can't do anything else"—as others do, with a prideful finality. No use trying to badger my kind into a confession that there are activities other than writing that we perform adequately or with comfort; we stand firm.

But when we say that we write because we can't do anything else, what do we actually mean? Do we mean that writing is the first impulse of all humans and that writers are humans too lazy to go on to the next step? Do we mean that writing is the one thing that every human can do and that every human would be a writer if he were not afflicted—or rescued, depending on your views—by other capacities? Do we mean that every particularly inept person "is" a writer?

Certainly not. The implication that's stuffed carelessly to the back of the formulation is that there's a specific sort of difference between writing and the anything else that we might be doing if we could do it—kayaking, decorating cakes, building bird feeders, operating oil refineries—some difference other than degree of developmental advancement.

Since there are few writers who can make a living on the strength of their writings, most of us simply must do something other than write. And of course there have always been writers with vast, demonstrable areas of competency—Anton Chekhov and Joseph Conrad spring easily to mind, but the instances are innumerable. Even the image, so cherished by many of us, of Franz Kafka tremblingly pitted against the demands of low-echelon office work is being revised. Now we're oppressed by the image of Kafka as a robust CEO, possessing appetites, business acumen, social fluency. The phenomenon of the abundantly gifted is another matter, though; and those for whom I take it upon myself to speak, or to speculate, are writers like me, who, whatever the quality of our writings, are actively bad at other things.

But if we're not even necessarily making a claim for the quality of the writings we produce, what is the thing we're claiming not to be bad at?

The act of writing itself, evidently—the very act of writing. So, then, what might be the act of writing? What are some of the things that writers are doing when they write that distinguish writing from all things that are not writing?

There is, most obviously, the business of fitting the inchoate and intractable plasma of sensation or experience into the brittle containers—words and grammatical forms—with which we convey it to the reader. Perhaps you'll object that this is not peculiar to writing, that this matching-up of substance and shape is in fact a precondition for one of the most fundamental human enterprises—conversation.

You'd be mistaken. Anyone who's had occasion to read a transcript of a conversation will have marveled that the parties involved could possibly have understood one another at all. The fact is that, *in situ*, people employ all manner of other vehicles of expression—gestures, faces, postures, tones—to get their meaning across when the words, racing by as they do, fail to do the job. Actually, if we're to be honest with ourselves, we have to admit that, more often than not, the meaning never exactly does come across. We adopt the expediency of believing that we understand one another in conversation; we have an impression of what was intended by others (and an impression of what we ourselves have intended) or we have a very general or approximate understanding of it. But no one could really understand precisely and in detail what is said in most conversations, because most conversations are ambiguous, allusive, and incoherent. If the same standards of clarity applied to writing, no one would read a thing.

In addition to the task of "putting things into words" and the problems that involves, there's the task that, if not exclusive to writing, is a task that writing always involves—discovering what it is that ought to get put into those words. Since we're speaking here particularly of fiction writers, we can call this "finding a story."

Happily, the human world is rich in stories. The newspaper rattles on in its exuberant way; the reader is riveted: We feel that we are—and it's true that we are—learning about life. Even those stories that seem similar to countless others never fail to fascinate us (often by their very predictability) when we read them in the newspaper or hear them on the phone from our friends or even watch one inexorably unfold at home from an inconsequential-looking little seed, turning our orderly lives into raging jungles.

But how rare it is to feel that we are learning about life when we read fiction! Actuality has a luster that fiction can rarely exceed, and that the fiction writer, in his respectful humility, rarely hopes to be able even to match. We know when we read or hear a "true" story that eventually, polishing and defining itself as it tumbles about in our brain with other "true" stories, it will yield up some shiny or weighty nugget. Almost any "true" story, however wandering or poorly told or incomplete, is revelatory simply because it (or something that corresponds roughly to the profile of its incidents) really occurred. Amazing, we think: *that* is a thing that reality can accommodate! *That* can *happen!*

But the unfortunate fiction writer can only say of the story he or she invents (or infers as a plausible expression of life's potentialities) "Well, but it *might* have happened" or "Those deeds entered my mind and I am a person, therefore those deeds can enter a person's mind, and once in a person's mind, they could be committed."

But *were* the deeds committed? Did the thing *actually happen?* No. Or if it did, if a particular story we read as fiction is a story taken from "real life," it's the writer who must abstract from the story its revelatory core. The marvel of the "true" story is its very arbitrariness: Why, we wonder, was *that* the particular thing that managed to fight its way to the top of the heap of all possibilities into actuality? But heaven forbid the fictional story is, or appears to be, either arbitrary or unlikely. If I present a "true" story in a work of fiction, I must illustrate that apart from the fact that the events *did* occur, they *could* have occurred, as well. And not only could they have occurred, but given the conditions I've posited, things could hardly have worked out in any other way.

So, why should anyone take the trouble to read, let alone write, fiction? Yeah, echoes the world, why? We have an ever-expanding sea of lurid biographies to splash around in—why should we bother with fake reality when we've got real reality?

Well, because fiction has other aims in view. Fiction is not—in its more ambitious aspects, at least—intended as a simulation of reality, although almost inevitably it embraces an exploration of reality, or what we experience as reality, and therefore *entails* a simulation of reality. Nonfiction depends on facticity; fiction depends on a different sort of truthfulness. The fiction writer must persuade us that, in one way or another, his or her story is accurate, whether it's a story of a man walking around Dublin or a story of a man waking up to find that he's a dung-beetle. But the convincingness of the story will rest not on the verifiability of the incidents, but in the integrity of their meaning. So, although the fiction writer must manage to simulate in some form, through enormous effort and ingenuity, what the nonfiction writer can simply present to us, he or she must accomplish something other than that as well. Where fiction relies on faithfulness to fact it must show us that what is interesting because it's true is also interesting because it's interesting; what is meaningful because it's true is also meaningful because it's meaningful. If fiction were only an inferior form of nonfiction, I'd happily agree that we could dispense with the whole troublesome business. But although the reader may derive similar pleasures from each, and although various technical difficulties of arranging information— for sense and for effect—may be common to both, fiction and nonfiction are deeply different sorts of enterprises.

Excellent fictional narratives fall into no particular categories, to my way of thinking, but perhaps something that can be said of all of them is that they convey an impression of inarguability. Occasionally one feels that the world or some particularly outstanding writer has offered up a story so pure in its lines, so ringing in its episodes, that it appears simply to have been observed and transcribed. *Anna Karenina,* for example, conveys the illusion of a line whose thrust is so inevitable that it would have been apparent to any bystander at its first point. *Madame Bovary,* another perfect narrative, seems on the other hand to have been solicited by a peculiar mind and tempered by a peculiar sensibility from what another observer might well have regarded as simply a sordid but ordinary chaos.

But whether a narrative appears to have been something that was just glowing there for anyone to see or to have been a fortunate combustion between one particular writer and one particular story, you can be sure that actually it cost the author a great deal of trouble to set that fictional chain of events into inexorable, blazing motion.

Perhaps it seems that all this is simply to say that writing takes time. And therefore since time is a medium in which activities compete, that simple logic will insist that writing is an activity that leaves writers little time to do other things, thus little time to do other things well.

But successful executives, for example, are portrayed as having *spare* time—time to go to the gym, to host dinner parties, to attend to the children, to do whatever time-consuming things they need to do to spend or protect all that money they've made during the rest of their time. Where does all this time come from? Executives surely have no more hours in a day than do writers. Are we to conclude, then, that executives are much more intelligent or energetic than writers, or that it simply takes more time to write a book than to run a company?

Actually, there are writers who require hardly more time to write something than to type it (although for most of us the differential is shocking, and would be practically beyond the credence of most readers, for whom, fortunately, the matter is of no interest), but the speed at which a writer works seems to have no particular bearing on his or her repertoire of capabilities; fast writers can be just as bad at things in general as slow writers.

If writing fiction were neither more nor less than fashioning into verbal form some pliant, proto-word-like material that's oozing around in our heads and selecting or isolating a hardy narrative, every writing endeavor would succeed in due course, and in a reliable, orderly manner. Writing would have to be seen largely as a series of mechanical challenges on the order of tool-and-die cutting. Undoubtedly more people would do it, and fewer people would want to do it.

But writing fiction is not orderly or reliable at all; I would imagine that every fiction writer has struggled with false starts and dead ends and characters who go their own merry ways, making all kinds of difficulties for their authors. So, in other words, there must be something else that impedes us from moving swiftly between the words *Chapter One* and the words *The End*. There must be some sort of difference between writing and other activities aside from "putting things into words" and "choosing a story"—one additional set of mental operations at least that prefigures or accompanies those.

The phrase "spending time" is illuminating, characterizing, as it does, the utilization of time as an economic transaction. We can readily see what the hypothetical executive above is getting in return for his or her expenditure (a superior body, a superior social life, superior children, and so on). But we might have to ask what, for a commensurate expenditure, the writer is getting.

In fact, the resemblance between writing and doing nothing at all can be striking, perhaps even profound. Sometimes, the piece of paper that was blank at breakfast is blank, still, by twilight. Worse, and more often, it will simply have been defaced by banalities.

A friend calls: What are you doing? Are you doing anything? Why not (for example) come watch me get my hair set?

Almost anything seems more dignified than that piece of paper, and it's the unusual writer who has the self-confidence—or self-importance—to answer time after time, all evidence to the contrary, I can't, I'm working.

Are we working? Hard to say. Should we eventually produce something that the world applauds (or even merely accepts), we have been "working." Should we produce nothing, or something we're willing to divulge only to the trash can, we have been "wasting time."

Writing fiction, because we never quite know what a particular endeavor is until we have completed it, has no discernible borders. Whether we're at the typewriter or in the tub, our minds are in some way at the service of the thing that's taking shape within them. In other words, everything we do, including nothing, might qualify equally well or poorly as work. And this continuous mental engagement is sustained by a complementary continuous mental resistance—a deep resistance to using time or thought in a pragmatic or efficient way, even a resistance to "word" and "story" themselves.

Readers sometimes say to writers, how did you think of that word? But, of course, thinking of the word, this word or that word, is never the problem; the problem is *resisting* the word that we first think of—the word we automatically use to indicate something—and to think instead of what the word (which we'll eventually be bound to then find) *means*. Something similar is true in regard to "story." The task is not primarily to "think up" a story, but to *penetrate* the story, to discard the elements of it that are merely shell, or husk—that give apparent form to the story but actually obscure its essence. In other words, the problem is to transcend the givens of a narrative.

It's quite usual when writing to discover that what seemed to be an inspiration is actually a platitude, to watch an idea degrade just as it unfolds, to have to write something ten, twenty, thirty times before all the clinging stupidities and excesses are purged from it and something bright and substantial emerges. Since I do a certain amount of teaching, I encounter young writers of real ability who, being unfamiliar with the amount of labor that writing something worthwhile requires from most of us, expect to be able to sit down and just ... write something worthwhile. Sometimes these inexperienced writers, in their dismay at the shortcomings of their initial efforts, adjust—to correspond to the quality of what they have produced—either their estimation of their abilities or their estimation of what is worthwhile writing. Either response is unfortunate: The first can be a personal disaster, the second a disaster for the culture—or part of the same disaster that has placed virtually every demanding or complex literary experience beyond our culture's confines.

It's one of the dominant, as well as more exasperating, elements of the art of writing to have to read what we are writing and ask ourselves if it is in any way truthful or accurate, to ask whether it actually represents what we want it to represent or whether it's an approximation, a cliché. It's simply amazing how resourceful the brain is in producing and interposing between us and our goal ever more adamant, ever more sophisticated clichés. It's as if the brain were leafletting for a hysterical candidate, as if it were designed to overcome our probings into it the way bacteria are designed to overcome the assaults of antibiotics.

In short, a very large part of what we do, a very large part of what "writing" is, is resistance—a process of scrutinizing and discarding the word, the narrative, the interpretation that comes easily to mind. On and off paper, writers tend to use their minds and their time to evade or subvert the terms in which they've been told to see what they see, and even the notion that they do see what they've been told they see. They must then use their minds and their time to avoid substituting in its place some artificial invention or construction of their own.

Sometimes people who don't know writers are astonished when they meet us because we can seem weirdly obtuse, or at least intellectually bizarre. There are those of us who have had to grow accustomed to the chilling stare that greets our offhand comments. There are those of us whose acquaintances, relatives, teachers, have expressed frequent incredulity—why are we so befuddled by some simple task; why do we nervously dwell on some negligible detail and fail to comprehend the important whole; why can we not be made to take seriously some issue of obvious seriousness, or why, conversely, do we take so seriously some obvious trifle?

I myself went through school without being able to understand most of what my teachers were trying to get across to me, or to retain it; the putative information just would not resolve itself into comprehensibility in my mind. It was as if I had shrunk to an infinitesimal size on a tablecloth—each space in the weave appeared to be an ocean, each thread a portion of a massive cable without beginning or end.

If I were several decades younger, no doubt my problems would have been classified as a severe learning disability. Though I'm sorrier than I can say that I learned so little, and I desperately wish I could now take a pill that would restore to me those lost increments of instruction, I'm just as glad to have escaped without either diagnosis or treatment.

Because, aside from the medical and social consequences of such an interpretation of my strange mental makeup, I suppose that if I had considered it to be an illness that could be cured, I might not have made the happy discovery eventually that it perfectly equipped me to write—or at least to write as I myself happen to write. I wouldn't dream of proposing that an evident dimness is the sine qua non of the working habits of all writers, but it certainly seems to be a sine qua non of mine. That is, I've not been able to understand things in the way I'm intended to understand them, so I've simply had to understand them in the way I've been able to understand them.

There are writers who are amazingly articulate in spontaneous speech—Samuel Johnson, Fran Lebowitz, Isaiah Berlin, to name a few of the more famously so; but it's sort of a joke among a lot of us how amazingly inarticulate we are. And really, when you think about what we're doing when we write, it's not that surprising that "um, er" is our customary contribution to a conversation.

Striving for finesse and specificity in his or her work, a fiction writer can hardly help cultivating a native penchant towards resistance and skepticism. The discipline that results can't necessarily be assumed by morning at the desk only to be discarded by evening at dinner. And what a good thing that is, because this same severity preserves the world in a fluid state, providing the writer with the freedom to experiment in aesthetic alchemy—often, of course, to horrible effect—to wander through dim, protean, unexplored corridors of the brain and to report back sightings of the human, as that animal lives privately and essentially, without the camouflage of proper clothing. What each fiction writer has to offer is only the way in which, with one particular brain, from one particular situation, one particular person sees whatever he or she sees. This application of idiosyncrasies of mind to human events is often an adjunct to what might be considered either crippling slow-wittedness or an abnormal velocity adequate to break the barriers of the received.

It's ludicrous as well as distasteful to speak of a life devoted to serious fiction writing as a "career." Whether it is done quickly or slowly, however splendid the results, the process of writing fiction is inherently, inevitably, indistinguishable from wasting time. Certainly, if you want to do almost anything well, confusion, incomprehension, anxiety, inefficiency, and the inappropriate response will hardly be advantageous. But for the fiction writer's trek through the wilderness, they might be considered quite a useful set of orientations.

WILLIAM LASHNER

The Writing Life

Ah, the writing life.

A few months ago I found myself on a small boat, about thirty miles due west of Assateague Island, hunting for tuna. This was my first attempt at sport fishing and I soaked it all in, the sun, the salt sea, lines like spider's silk slipping from the boat into the dark roiling ocean. Beneath us a lovely silver ghost, all power and grace, slid low through the blackness. In the offing was a battle against nature, a test of wills between man and fish. It was all too exquisite until, with an ominous snap, the reel on one of the rods started whizzing.

An hour later, my biceps burning, my wrist aching, my bones turned to taffy by exhaustion, the rod yanked me once again across the deck, already slippery thick with a crimson red slop. I tripped over a fish still flopping away on the boards, a fish bigger than my eldest child, and banged my hip into the rail. The rod slipped in my hands, I barely maintained my grip.

"Face the fish," drawled the mate.

"How far is he?" I gasped.

"Oh you got a ways to go. We've snagged our limit, anyways, so we'll have to throw it back."

"Throw it back?"

The rod jerked, my hands burned, the fish made another run, and line fled from the reel. I stepped over dead tuna as the bluefin worked me back and forth across the deck, my muscles ripping off the elbow, my feet slipping in the blood, my seasick patch shaking loose.

Through it all one thought kept hammering at my skull: Hemingway was a jerk.

So maybe I wasn't born for the hard-living manly writer's life. Maybe driving to Key West I would find myself, not reborn, just carsick. Maybe I'm more of an open the can, add mayonnaise and a touch of dill kind of guy. I mean, I figure if it's laughs I'm after I might as well step inside a cage of ropes and let some guy with the shoulders of a bull bash me in the face.

Oh yeah, he did that, too.

My run at sport fishing wasn't the only time my dreams of the writing life had withered in the face of abject reality. Much of what I had hoped for when I decided on a writing career in my adolescence, the joyous nights of drink, the fame, the easy sex, the jazz bars, the place in the Hamptons, the easy sex, the prime table at Elaine's, all of it has seemed to pass me by.

I'm not complaining now; it's just that these images of the writing life, images that sparked my early desire to write and drove me though the Iowa Writer's Workshop and my family into debt until finally I sold a novel on my third attempt, have proven to be largely illusory. I always considered those who said they wouldn't let success change their lives to be a bit daft—if success doesn't change things, then what's the point of all this confounded striving. I thought when that first book came out everything would be different, that the very earth would shift on its axis and I would be reborn, but here I am, same as I ever was, and my life is remarkably unchanged. Same house, same wife, same way I have to jiggle that knob to make the toilet flush. What could be more disappointing? In fact, only one aspect of the writer's life hasn't disappointed, only one aspect has far exceeded all my adolescent yearnings.

• • •

When I decided to stop talking about being a writer and try to actually do something about it, the writing itself was this unpleasant thing I forced upon myself with the hope of someday living the life to which we all aspire. I would dream the parties, the money, the summers on Sidney Sheldon's yacht, and then chain myself to the typewriter to hammer out still another limp page. I finished a novel that way, well, if not a novel at least a long glob of glutinous prose, forced myself to finish it and then sent it off, eyeing the catalogues for cruise wear as I waited for the life to descend upon me.

It didn't.

So I'm sitting home, alone, watching reruns of *F-Troop*, when a voice comes out of my television and asks if I am desperate for a change. Of course I am desperate for a change. Who watching reruns of *F-Troop* isn't desperate for a change? The answer, says the voice, is career training, and right there it offers certifications in Legal Assistant, Medical Assistant, Taxidermy, Creative Writing, Prisoner Execution, Driver Education Film Narration. The Taxidermy class was filled, so I opted for creative writing, which is how I ended up in Iowa, going for my MFA.

I had never before taken a writing class and at the start I wrote like they tell you to drive, defensively. I carefully drafted a passel of short stories designed in their utter blandness to avoid the withering criticism of my workshop classmates and teachers. I wrote for approval and failed, spectacularly. Battered and bloody, oh the humanity, I gave up on short fiction and embarked upon another novel. I used to run cross country, pitifully of course—the bus, fully loaded, engine running, waiting for me to finish—but still I figured I was better suited to the longer track. Slowly, page by painful page, the manuscript grew. Then, strangely, something totally unexpected happened. The damn thing spoke to me.

"I'm not sure I like the direction in which you're heading," it said.

"Be quiet."

"Don't you think you should emphasize the father's role in Lee's life?"

"I think I emphasized it enough."

"But isn't the struggle being waged for his soul really between his father and Hal? Shouldn't that be the emphasis of the story?"

"What the hell do you know about it?"

Now you might think that I'm making it up, this conversation, having a jolly joke on myself and my book, but here's the thing, I'm not, it happened—the damn thing spoke to me, and it took a long time for me to get smart enough to listen. Joseph Campbell says in *The Power of Myth* that every artist feels the work speak to him and if cave drawings could speak to the Neanderthal painter then I suppose my manuscript could indeed speak to me. In fact, it was only when I smartened up enough to listen that the voice of my narrator came alive, the story began to drive itself, and the act of writing ceased to be a painful obligation. My favorite part of the Iowa day was no longer the softball games with famous writers or the talk of writing over beers at the Foxhead or the poker, it was, instead, time with my ever-lengthening novel. And I knew then that I wanted to continue to hear that voice forever.

The voice doesn't make itself heard at the start, no matter how detailed the notes I've generated. I have to slog a bit, waiting for the manuscript to start whispering in my ear. It seems to come, when it does, about a hundred pages in, and those hundred pages are hard, full of doubts and thoughts of other more worthy projects. Sometimes it comes sooner or sometimes later or sometimes never at all, in which case I put it away and start something new, and sometimes what it tells me is that the first hundred pages are a disaster. When I start, it is an act of faith, hoping it will come, not certain that it will but certain that if I don't begin it won't ever. And when it does come, too soft to hear at first, a mere murmur that slips into my dreams, but then louder and more insistent, it brings with it not merely its own voice but an entire world, the world of my fiction. It is only when the novel

starts to speak that I know the world of the manuscript has somehow come alive for me, and with the coming of the voice that
world itself inhabits me in a peculiar way even as I continue to
create its contours.

It has become for me an exquisitely private pleasure, this habi-
tation by the dreamworlds of my novels, a pleasure that grows
more powerful with each book. I find myself slipping into the
worlds not just when I'm writing, but at odd moments during the
other parts of my life, at a concert, during a long drive, while discussing a stain with the dry cleaner. At night, before I fall asleep, I
spend my last moments awake lost in thoughts of my writing, and
so my first moments of sleep are spent in those dreamworlds, too.
They are worlds with a surface comprised of words and if there is
a distortion in my view it can usually be traced to an imprecise
verb, a metaphor that dies, a rhythm in the sentence that clangs.
Language haunts my sleep; phrases bubble up through my
dreams and I fight to reconstruct the precise wording when I
awake. If there is a terror alongside the pleasure in these dreams it
is that my language will ultimately fail my vision.

I would have expected the worlds of my stories to be foreign,
filled with landmarks and characters that I have only recently
sketched with words, but I find I am not an alien in these places.
Over there, that man on the crowded urban street with the
slightly stooped walk. His name is Martin and he is someone
whom I made up out of the thin of the air, an old socialist rabble-
rouser, a devoted follower of Eugene Debs, but when he turns
and looks at me I recognize him for who he really is, my father.
And that house, that split level squatting on that hillside plot,
doesn't that look a little like the suburban split level in which I
spent my early youth? I can write about a gothic mansion in
Philadelphia's Main Line or a German immigrant neighborhood
in turn-of-the-century Cincinnati or Paris during the occupation
and, somehow, the psychological profile of the worlds will all feel
startlingly familiar, as if I had spent my whole life there and no

place else but there. Look, within that large dormitory room at a Nazi run internment camp for Jews just outside Paris, sitting on one of the flea-ridden straw mattresses, a man, stooped and thin, patiently awaiting his fate. Is that my father again?

It is impossible to explain how lovely it is to lose myself in the dreamworlds of my novels, how delicious. I used to let others look at sections of my books before I was finished—I have the writer's pathetic need for approval, so similar to a dog's—but though I still have that need, I don't show works in progress anymore; the readers always feel obligated to give their opinions, why else of course would I show it, and I don't want their voices to still the voice of the manuscript. So I work alone to the end and rewrite and rewrite again alone until I think it is ready and all the time my visits to the world are absolutely private. It is my world, separate from the other world, mine and only mine, a place of solace and refuge where everything wrong can be rewritten right unless I like it exactly wrong. In times of stress I enter it and lie down in its green pastures and let it restoreth my soul. There is something selfish about my visits that adds to the pleasure, gives it a tinge of guilt, like having an intense extramarital affair while retaining absolute fidelity to my family. It is mine, this dreamworld, until I'm finished with the story and I send it away and it is solely mine no longer, and somehow, in the sharing, the voice quiets and the world begins to dissolve and disappear for me, like a dream upon waking. It becomes something fixed and hard and different. When I complete a book I am supposed to be happy, relieved. I am supposed to rejoice that I am finished, but what I feel more than anything is loss. When I turn in a manuscript for the final time it is as if, in the garden of my novel, I have eaten from the fruit of completion and, as punishment, been banished.

My professional life is now divided into two distinct parts. There is the writing itself, which, as I've described, is difficult and magical and something I hope to do for as long as I have the strength. And there is the other stuff that comes with publication, the expected writerly stuff, the sport fishing as it were, which I do, gladly, with a song in my heart, but only because it is what I have to do so that they'll let me keep writing.

I have my picture taken, I am interviewed over the phone, I make the occasional appearance on cable television and regale the audience with clever self-deprecating anecdotes. I travel all over the country, signing books at tables in malls. I give readings and answer questions and am amazingly grateful to anyone who takes the time to show up and listen. At my hotel I order room service and call my wife and watch HBO and sleep through the night without a child waking me with a request for water, which is actually lonelier than I ever would have imagined. I contact friends I haven't seen in years and we have lunch. I call my publicist to keep him informed of my progress. I am reviewed.

Of course I had my dreams of waiting up all night at a publication party, drinking champagne with starlets, expecting any moment the messenger bearing the next morning's papers so that we can read together the grand reviews of my latest. "Here it is, here it is," says my agent after frantically searching through the paper. "Is it good?" asks the starlet. "Good?" shouts my agent. "It's better than good, it's boffo." Of course the reality of reviews turned out to be still another disappointment. Being reviewed is like being workshopped by the entire country while you stand in front of the class, naked. For me, actually, it's not the criticism that I find most unpleasant, though even a few snide words cause a pain so brutal, so unyielding, that thoughts of sweet homicide begin to infect my thoughts day and night, night and day, until I find myself loitering outside gun shops and apothecaries specializing in exotic poisons, but, really, the criticism is not the worst part. The worst part of the reviews for me is when the reviewers begin to describe the story, to distill the novel's world down to the banal few sentences that fit within their allotted column inches, taking all the quirks of architecture and character out of it, until it is almost a parody of what I intended to write. Yet the characters' names are the same and some events are the same and, yes, they seem to have gotten the basics right, but, no, it is nothing like the dream I had slipped in and out of the last two years. That, more than anything, makes me feel a failure and, somehow, drives me to find the lost world again in another incarnation in another book in hopes that I might do a better job.

I haven't given up all aspirations to the glorious fun I had lusted for as a boy. I remember reading how Fitzgerald and Faulkner and Dorothy Parker prostituted themselves to Hollywood and my first thought was, "How wasteful," and my second thought was, "How about me?" Someday soon I'll head out to the coast and stand on a street corner in a bad Hawaiian shirt, flashing leg and manuscript, holding a sign: "Will rewrite wrestling film for dinner at Morton's." I'm sure it will be fab and wild and nothing like I had hoped, and I'll be glad as hell to get back home to start again and lose myself in a novel.

A room of my own, an idea with promise, two years to flesh out its world.

Ah, the writing life.

FRANCINE PROSE

On Details

Some years ago I heard a true story I found disturbing, puzzling, and weirdly cheering, because it is partly about the power of storytelling—and the power of detail. This story, which, to tell the truth, I have never entirely understood, was told to me by a friend whose life in art has mostly involved telling versions of his true-life story, and who was hired by Esalen, the venerable New Age institute in Big Sur, California, to lead a workshop on the subject of telling true-life stories. The purpose of the workshop, as I understand it, was to help the participants (who had been admitted on the basis of letters demonstrating that each did indeed have a true-life story to tell) tell their true-life stories better.

On the first day of class my friend asked for a volunteer, and a woman raised her hand. As soon as she began to speak, my friend remembered her letter. This was a woman who had lost one leg to a bout with childhood cancer, but who recovered and had gone on to become a world-class downhill skiing champion. Her story was an account of her loss and her triumph, not just over one illness, but over several life-threatening diseases that left her not only unbowed and undefeated but progressively stronger. In fact she made her living as a motivational trainer, revving up burned-out salesmen and sluggish CEOs with a message of encourage-

ment based on her own experience, a message that could be sum-
marized as: I did this, so you can do that.

When she finished, my friend asked if she didn't ever want to
just go somewhere and scream. The woman said no, she did not,
she had no interest in screaming—in fact it was important to her
not to get in touch with what she called "her dark side."

On the second day of class, one of the male students volunteered to begin. This was a former investment broker or former
insider trader, someone who had earned millions and then given
up his meteoric career in high finance to attend spiritual workshops and courses all over California. He waited until the room
was silent and then announced, in a sort of growl, "I like to eat
pussy." As the beginning of a story—or whatever—it cut to the
chase, conveying swiftly and well the fact that the story he
intended to tell was meant to be not only confessional and pornographic, but also combative and aggressive.

He proceeded to tell an extremely confessional, pornographic,
and (my friend said) aggressive story about his sex life with his
wife. My friend spared me the details but said the story was so
well told that he couldn't move—he hardly breathed—the whole
time the man was talking. When he finished, the class was dead
silent, and my friend, not knowing what else to do, took what he
called the "technical route" and told the man that his story had
been very well told indeed.

At this point, the class went wild; many of the students were
furious, especially the women, who each in turn tried to explain
why she was so upset, how she'd experienced the story not only as
pornography (a subject about which the women in fact had
widely divergent views) but as simple aggression. It says something about manners, about the psychology of taboo, of sex and
of confession that it would have been considered permissible (in
some cases even sympathetic) for him to tell a story about system-
atically or accidentally tormenting his wife, but outrageous to
describe having raucous sex with her in many unlikely, risky, and

downright uncomfortable settings, though I suppose you can't blame the students for objecting to paying Esalen tuition to find themselves functioning as unpaid phone-sex workers.

The storyteller had meant to stir up the class and make extra work for the teacher. Now he sat back with his arms crossed: smiling, satisfied, delighted. On the third day of class, the one-legged woman asked if she could tell another story. She said that it was a confession—a version of her life that she'd told no one but her therapist. But the truth was: She'd lied on the first day, about how she'd lost her leg. The real story involved her sister, a deeply wicked and depraved person, and her sister's black cat, which—when the storyteller was a child—bit her on the leg: a wound she refused to attend to, and which subsequently became infected, and festered.

One night at family dinner—always a tense occasion, because their father was a passionate carnivore and their mother a strict vegetarian—the father began to rant and rave, yelling that the dining room stunk to high heaven, and it was the mother's tofu that smelled. Of course it wasn't the bean curd, but rather the daughter's leg, which had become gangrenous and had to be amputated.

Dear reader, you may at this moment be having doubts about this story, as I did—but my friend assured me that the woman told it with unwavering conviction, and that there wasn't one person in the room who didn't believe every word she said.

When the woman finished her story, no one spoke for a very long time. Then the woman confessed that she'd invented the story about the cat, that this second recounting of her misfortune was a complete fabrication—a revelation that the others accepted with a mixture of amazement, chagrin, humor, and good grace.

All, that is, except for the man who'd told the pornographic story. He rose to his feet and said that he felt that they'd been had, tricked, hoodwinked—and frankly he didn't like it. Furthermore, he said that my friend—that is, the workshop leader—was nothing but a bad actor. He left the classroom, left Esalen—and was never heard from again.

Not since Scheherazade saved her life by telling her spouse the tales from the Arabian Nights in enthralling serial installments has there been such conclusive proof of the power of fiction. How oddly brave the woman was to use a story—and her disability—as a heat-seeking missile, a perfectly and accurately aimed weapon of retaliation. (The part that I don't claim to understand is how she could have known how well her plan would work—or that it would work at all.)

The reason I've told this story is not to horrify or disturb the reader with its horrifying and disturbing aspects, or even to encourage those of us (myself included) who have been laboring away in solitude in our studies and garrets, wondering if our fiction means anything or can do anything, if anyone really cares ... but because of something my friend said. He told me that the whole reason the class believed the woman's story—a loopy Gothic tall tale about a gangrenous cat bite—was entirely because of the detail about the father's love for steak and the mother's devotion to tofu.

"Trust me on this," my friend said. "God really is in the details."

If God is in the details, we all must on some deep level believe that the truth is in there, too, or maybe it is that God is truth: Details are what persuade us that someone is telling the truth—a fact that every liar knows instinctively and too well. Bad liars pile on the facts and figures, the corroborating evidence, the improbable digressions ending in blind alleys, while good or (at least better) liars know that it's the single priceless detail that jumps out of the story and tells us to take it easy, we can quit our dreary adult jobs of playing judge and jury and again become as trusting children, hearing the gospel of grown-up knowledge without a single care or doubt.

What a relief it is when a detail reassures us that a writer is in control and isn't putting us on. Let's say we're a little ... uncertain about Gregor Samsa waking up from a night of disturbing dreams to find himself changed in his bed into a giant beetle. Kafka tells us, "It was no dream," but why should we believe him? The facts of insect anatomy—of Gregor's hard, armor-plated back, his rounded brown belly divided in segments, his numerous sticklike legs, waving helplessly in the air above him—are painfully convincing, but still we could be reading the script for a Japanese monster movie or a passage of science fiction by a brilliant but demented beginning writer. It isn't until Gregor surveys his room that we lose our last shred of suspicion that this might be a dream and know that this can only be the real world of great fiction.

> **Above the table on which a collection of cloth samples was unpacked and spread out—Samsa was a commercial traveler—hung the picture which he had recently cut out of an illustrated magazine and put into a pretty gilt frame. It showed a lady, with a fur cap on and a fur stole, sitting upright and holding out to the spectator a huge fur muff into which the whole of her forearm had vanished!**

This picture is the perfect detail and has all the qualities of the perfect detail: it is at once surprising, unexpected, inventive, unpredictable, but entirely plausible, serious but somehow playful, apt—but not in the least heavy-handed or pointedly symbolic. The magazine picture of the lady in furs is exactly the sort of thing that, we imagine, a commercial traveler might choose to brighten up his bachelor's bedroom. And believing in this picture, we begin to believe in Gregor and in the possibility that he could turn into a bug. (Also, this detail combines a convincingly nervy mix of irony and plausibility, since the daring sub-detail of the hand disappearing into the fur muff is almost too perfect to find in the room of a man who is already having a bit of a problem with anatomical boundaries and species identification.)

Great and merely very good writers, the living and the dead, painstakingly construct their fictions with small but significant details that, brushstroke by brushstroke, paint the pictures the artists hope to portray, the strange or familiar realities of which they hope to convince us: details of landscape and nature (the facts of marine and whale biology in *Moby-Dick*), of weather (the falling snow at the end of James Joyce's "The Dead"), details of fashion (the tailor's dummies in Bruno Schulz, the snake-colored green-and-yellow dress in Chekhov's "In the Ravine," the hospital bracelets that the customers of the loser's bar are still wearing in Denis Johnson's "Jesus's Son"), details of home decoration (the ancient wedding cake in Miss Havisham's room, the peacocks and the mold of the wife's teeth on top of the TV in Raymond Carver's "Feathers"), details of speech and gesture (Madame Bovary turning her face to the wall when she learns she's given birth to a girl), of food (Proust's madeleine), details of botany (Colette's mother's sedum plant blooming once every how-many years), details of music (the Kreutzer Sonata in the eponymous Tolstoy novella), of basketball, auto mechanics, of all the things with which we humans express our hopes and fears, our complex individuality.

Even those writers we may consider above or beyond detail, those who seem more concerned with oddities of language and aberrant states of consciousness than with creating naturalistic scenes and plausible dialogue, even Samuel Beckett wrote—in almost the same words Chekhov used half a century earlier—"In the particular is contained the universal." The details of the sixteen sucking stones Molloy transfers from pocket to pocket as he tries to suck each one equally and the crutches he ties to his bicycle rise like sharp peaked islands out of that bleak and hilarious great dismal swamp of a novel.

Like many writers, Chekhov filled his notebook not only with large observations about philosophy and life in general—ideas of the sort that never appear in his stories except in the mind of a character, the pompous, the self-deluded, the disappointed, or the hopeful about to be disappointed—but also with minute trivia of the sort that might have actually made it into one of his stories or plays: "A bedroom. The light of the moon shines so brightly through the window that even the buttons on his night shirt are visible" and "a tiny little schoolboy with the name of Tractenbauer." His letters stress the importance of the single, well-chosen detail:

> In my opinion a true description of nature should be very brief and have the character of relevance. Commonplaces such as "the setting sun bathed the waves of the darkening sea, poured its purple gold, etc.," "the swallows flying over the surface of the water tittered merrily"—such commonplaces one ought to abandon. In descriptions of nature one ought to seize upon the little particulars, grouping them in such a way that, in reading, when you shut your eyes you get the picture.
>
> For instance you will get the full effect of a moonlit night if you write that on the milldam, a little glowing starpoint flashed from the neck of a broken bottle, and the round black shadow of a dog or a wolf emerged and ran, etc. . . .
>
> In the sphere of psychology, details are also the thing. God preserve us from commonplaces. Best of all is to avoid depicting the hero's state of mind; you ought to try to make it clear from the hero's actions.

We cannot think of Chekhov's stories without thinking of their details: The most famous, I suppose, is the slice of watermelon that Gurov cuts and eats in Anna Sergeyevna's hotel room, but there is also the way that the bishop's old mother (in "The Bishop"), who has come to see her son, pushes a wine glass and a tumbler away from her granddaughter, Katya, so the child won't break a glass in the bishop's presence. This single true gesture obviates pages of psychological exposition describing how awed and uneasy the old woman feels around the son who has grown away from her to become an important man in the church, a gesture and a set of emotions given another spin by the fact that the bishop is dying. . . .

Some of his lesser stories have the most stunning details—for example, the details of the ironing board, the iron, and the boiled potato in the climactic scene of "The Murder." As the scene begins, Matvey, a poor factory worker and a religious fanatic, has been arguing about money and religion with his cousin Yakov, a poor tavern-owner and another sort of religious fanatic. Matvey has been living in the tavern with Yakov, Yakov's wife, and their retarded daughter, Dashutka, all of whom hate Matvey, and all of whom he hates.

> **Then Matvey went into the kitchen and began peeling some boiled potatoes which he had probably put away from the day before.**

A page later, Yakov has gone through a brief but hysterical spiritual crisis on the theme of faith and doubt and repentance, and we again catch up with Matvey, "sitting in the kitchen before a bowl of potato, eating. . . . Beneath the stove and the table at which Matvey was sitting was stretched an ironing board; on it stood a cold iron."

Matvey asks Yakov's wife Aglaia for a little oil to put on his potatoes, a simple enough request except that this is Lent and oil, apparently, is one of the things restricted by the fast. Yakov screams that Matvey can't have oil, they call each other heretics and sinners, order each other to repent, a scuffle ensues, and Yakov's wife, thinking her husband is in danger, picks up the bottle of oil,

> **. . . and with all her force brought it down straight on the skull of the cousin she hated. Matvey reeled, and in one**

instant his face became calm and indifferent. Yakov, breathing heavily, excited and feeling pleasure at the gurgle the bottle had made, like a living thing, when it had struck the head, kept him from falling and several times (he remembered this very distinctly) motioned Aglaia towards the iron with his finger; and when only the blood began trickling from his hands and he heard Dashutka's loud wail, and Matvey rolled heavily on it, Yakov left off his anger and understood what had happened.

"Let him rot." Agalia cried, still with the iron in her hand. The white bloodstained kerchief slipped on to her shoulders and her grey hair fell in disorder. "He's got what he deserved!"

Everything was terrible. Dashutka sat on the floor near the stove with the yarn in her hands, sobbing, continually bowing down, uttering at each bow a gasping sound. But nothing was so terrible to Yakov as the potato in the blood, on which he was afraid of stepping, and there was something else terrible which weighed upon him like a bad dream and seemed the worst danger, though he could not take it in for a minute. This was the waiter, Sergy Nikanoritch, who was standing in the doorway with the reckoning beads in his hand, very pale, looking with horror at what was happening in the kitchen.

"We think in generalities," wrote Alfred North Whitehead. "But we live in detail." To which I would add: We remember in detail, we recognize in detail, we identify, we recreate. Cops rarely ask eyewitnesses for general vague descriptions of the perpetrator. Recently my son was trying to remember a Greek myth in school and kept referring to the story about the pomegranate seeds until at last we deciphered that he meant the story of Persephone: Forget being kidnapped by Pluto, forget the half-life in the Underworld, the months underground, forget the mother's grief intense enough to darken the natural world. It was a story about a detail that I myself had forgotten: The number of months that Persephone agreed to spend with her husband underground was determined by a test that had something to do with the number of pomegranate seeds she ate. (Actually, one characteristic of the skilled teacher is a sharp awareness of the student's natural appetite for narrative and detail. My son's sixth-grade class all became fervent Caravaggio fans after their teacher told them how the painter killed a man in a fight after a tennis game.)

Reading the highly skilled, competent, but less than first-rate writer, we may vividly remember one detail from a novel but not the rest of the book—or even its title. So we may recall the scene from an Elmore Leonard thriller in which Teddy Majestyk's mother feeds her parrot with food from her mouth without being able to remember if this was the book in which so many characters seem to get pushed from high windows. Yet this selective memory can occur even in the case of a masterpiece: So we may retain only a vague sense of the shape of Turgenev's "First Love" and yet recall precisely the detail of the whip with which the narrator sees his father strike his young mistress on the arm.

If we doubt for one minute how our memory for detail can be trusted and relied on and played with and used to pull us though a story, consider the detail of Julian's mother's hat in Flannery O'Connor's "Everything That Rises Must Converge":

> **It was a hideous hat. A purple velvet flap came down on one side of it and stood up on the other; the rest of it was green and looked like a cushion with the stuffing out.**

Again, it is the perfect detail, the perfect hat for Julian's mother, and just like her (as Julian decides) "less comical than jaunty and pathetic." All her hopes and her soul are concentrated in that hat, all her desperate efforts to maintain some pretense of style and social standing, to present herself as an aristocrat come down in the world and forced to live among the peasants, the proud grand-daughter of a man who had a plantation with two-hundred slaves who were "better off" than the black people with whom she must now ride the bus to her reducing class at the Y and who, she thinks, "should rise, yes, but on their own side of the fence."

A bit later in the story our attention is again directed to "the preposterous hat" she wears "like a banner of her imaginary dig-nity." So of course when a black woman gets on the bus in a "hideous hat. A purple velvet flap came down on one side of it and stood up on the other; the rest of it was green and looked like a cushion with the stuffing out," we get the significance of the coincidence a few moments before "the vision of the two hats, identical, broke upon [Julian] with the radiance of a brilliant sun-rise. His face was suddenly lit up with joy. He could not believe that Fate had thrust upon his mother such a lesson."

The details are what stick with us, as I realized recently after watch-ing a remarkable documentary called *Mob Stories,* a film in which each of five Mafiosi told, in turn, the story of his career in crime. Each story was preceded by a title—"Family," "Mutiny," "Revenge," etc.

Afterwards, I recalled the following details. Trying to explain how "sick" his boss was, one man said that his boss used to read about serial killers and be very impressed by how the guy had got-ten away with whacking twenty-eight people. "I mean, you hang around with wise guys, you never hear no one admiring serial killers. . . ." A Rodney Dangerfield look-alike served as the lawyer for himself and his friends and won the case by endearing himself to the jury with dirty jokes about his wife. Now he is back in jail on another charge, and the camera showed this big man grace-fully doing tai chi exercises in the prison garden.

The last narrator told the story of how he used to do terrible things to ingratiate himself with the big guys for whom he worked as a low-level debt collector. At forty, he fell in love and got married, had two kids, and redirected his life; he raised a quarter million to buy his way out of the mob and is now a born-again preacher.

The detail he kept returning to was the worst thing he used to do: He'd chain a guy, some deadbeat, to the back bumper of his car, and drag him along the street. The storyteller repeated this detail three times, I think, clearly amazed by his previous self, by the other life he used to lead, and with that edge of longing that always goes right along with nostalgia. And it was this detail—the man, the chain, the bumper—that made me believe every word of this guy's story of sin and repentance.

Reading back through the pages I've written, I must say I'm appalled by the details I've chosen for an essay about details: a one-legged skier, a gangrenous cat bite, a game of dueling stories, a cutout magazine photo beside the bed of a giant insect, a bloody potato on the kitchen floor, a wise guy driving down the road with a deadbeat tied to his bumper.

But really, why should I be surprised? Details aren't only the building blocks with which a story is put together. They're also clues to something deeper and wider and broader, to our subconscious—our squalling, impolite id bubbling thickly up to the surface.

There is one more detail, one final detail, that I feel I should add. Several months after the Esalen workshop ended, and a few weeks before my friend told me the story of the dueling stories, he'd gotten a letter from the woman—the one-legged champion skier. She wrote that for New Year's she had gone out into the desert and thrown back her head and just screamed and screamed and screamed, and she wanted to tell him that, and to say that she felt much better.

ELIZABETH McCRACKEN

Lottery Ticket

The central trauma of my childhood was this: I wanted to play the French horn, and my mother wouldn't let me.

She said I was too small, and I can't be certain that this wasn't part of the appeal: I knew it would be a good sight gag. Still, my parents forbade so little (Barbie dolls, too, though I feel less traumatized about that lack) that it rankled me. Maybe my mother was unwilling to sink the money into a French horn, because besides being small and therefore puny of lung, I had not previously displayed any musical talent whatsoever. From the earliest age, at dance lessons, I boogied to the beat of a different drummer, one who was having a seizure but wailed away with one stick anyhow. I could not carry a metal song with magnet gloves. I couldn't even remember song lyrics and could be heard to sing:

> *It had to be you,*
> *It had to be yoo-o-oo,*
> *It had to be you, it had to be you, it had to be*
> *(bomp! bomp!)*
> *yoo-oo-oo!*

Instead of a horn, I received a flute. I didn't like my flute, but that doesn't explain why, after four years of lessons, I was still incapable of playing anything except "Oats Peas Beans and Barley Grow."

Wait. Earlier than this, I had a *Wizard of Oz* poster that frightened me terribly. Also, as a very young child, I was nervous to the point of superstition around flushing toilets.

In other words, I will not be writing a memoir soon, thinly veiled as fiction or otherwise. (Possible titles: *No Daddy, Don't Flush!* or *Not Like Other Little Girls: My Lifelong Search for Barbie.*) My childhood I remember as several years of bad puns, tuna-fish casseroles, and long car trips. Barbieless, sure. Empty of oom-pa-pa. Toilets everywhere. Oddly enough, though, happy even so. The misfortunes I remember were entirely my own fault: I was a clumsy and willful child. At four, I turned on the stove, waited until it got red hot, and set my hand down upon it. I did plenty of similar things—my parents never told me I was a clumsy and willful child; they just told me to keep away from the stove thereafter—but I never did enough damage to spin into a good short story. My childhood (like, I fear, my fiction) was long on character, short on plot.

Nevertheless, I don't remember much playing at pretend. I did not have imaginary friends. I did not long to be a princess. My brother is fond of pointing out that when I was given a baby doll, I named her after myself and loved her very much. As a child, I was not a very imaginative person. It's true even now. Once I'm given an idea, I can run with it, but I don't think I could write either science fiction or magic realism at gunpoint. There's just too much to make up.

A would-be writer is supposed to have either a rich inner life or a rich outer one. I had neither. Still, I had to get material from someplace, and so I stole it, piecemeal, from my family.

Desiderata, I learned in library science school, were the items you needed for an archive to make it useful. Useful, not complete, because there is no such thing as a complete archive. There's always a letter out there you want and need, either in someone else's collection or in an attic or just unfound. You need and want things you don't even know exist. That's how collections work.

I have a family archive, of sorts, incomplete and overflowing. My family leaves a fine paper trail. Diaries and letters and comic sketches, poems and letters to God. My grandmother Jacobson had eleven brothers and sisters, some who wrote to her often and some just now and then. And the diplomas! My relatives completed courses of study the way some families go through fortunes or first wives. I love anything touched by my family, my best, most beloved, most unreliable narrators.

For instance: I have The Martha Archives. My mother and her twin sister were sickly kids, and Martha was hired as a baby nurse and stayed in the family's employ until the twins were five. Eventually she got married and moved on, sort of, but she never had children of her own, and she never forgot the twins. I liked my mother's Martha stories. Even after the girls were grown, Martha baked a sunshine cake—an angel food made with egg yolks instead of whites—and sent one half to each twin. She wrote often, at length, fondly. My mother, who says she had the happiest childhood on record, remembers Martha and her letters as pleasant and slightly daffy. My aunt Carolyn says the letters were dark and Dickensian, longing for a time that never really existed. "She said things like, 'I wish you were a baby again, so I could hold you in my arms,'" Aunt Carolyn told me, and shivered.

I'd always figured that the letters were somewhere in between: odd, possibly inappropriate, but not sinister. Later, I found a bunch of letters from Martha to my grandmother (she baby-sat while Grandmother went on business trips). Well, Martha, I thought, at last we meet.

Those were some of the creepiest letters I ever read. You could see how much Martha loved the girls, and you could see that the depth of feeling was not mutual. Martha was always assuring my grandmother that everything was fine, and that The Dollies—as she called the twins—didn't miss their mother at all. Martha's interest in The Dollies toilet-training was as impassioned as other people's interest in World War II: It was terrible and thrilling and certainly it would come out all for the best, but when, when? Martha invited The Dollies over for dinner at her mother's farm and let them play with the bunny before dinner. The main course: Bunny. She felt the girls were a little sensitive, to cry the way they did.

I can't decide how happy I am to know Martha's nature this well. I am glad to tease my mother, the world's greatest optimist, with stories of her youth: The Night She Was a Big Girl, All Night Long. But (as I am my mother's daughter) I regret that I can no longer think the best of Martha.

Still and of course, I wrote a story about it.

My older brother, Harry, once expressed interest in a chip that could be implanted in the brain in order to record, like a video camera, everything that ever happened to you. That way, if you wanted to know what your first day of kindergarten looked like, you could just watch it. Your sixteenth birthday, your college cross-country trip—all of it would be available for easy viewing. He didn't think such a chip was an entirely good idea, but there would be plenty he'd want to look at.

I told him I couldn't think of anything worse. There isn't a single factual frame I'd want to review. "Nothing?" he asks. Nothing at all.

We both think the other person isn't sentimental enough. My brother—who says that the only real trauma of *his* life was attending a party and learning that Spanky McFarland of *The Little Rascals* had just left—would love to be able to see what he experienced as a kid, to relive it. When he recently visited Portland, Oregon, our childhood home, he toured all the old sights and took photographs. Even better, if he could compare them to their late 1960s' selves, all that lost neon and cheap ice cream.

Whereas I'm so sentimental I don't want to know the truth. I love my misconceptions, my long-harbored grudges, my inexplicable fondnesses for people I haven't seen in years. What if I've been wrong all these years? What if I've misremembered? I don't want to know what it's really been like to be me.

Still, I do want to know what it was like to be Martha, and the chip in Martha's brain would show only the following: the little girls frolic with the bunny, the little girls are called in for dinner, the little girls are confused about the odd entree, the little girls burst into tears. The chip would miss Martha's consternation, and that's what I'm interested in, that's what I get from her letter. Hadn't she raised The Dollies to be practical? It was wartime, after all, and that rabbit was a treat, both as playmate and supper. Onscreen: the world rocking gently as Martha shakes her head. Inside: the disappointment that causes the shaking, the realization that despite her best intentions, she's guessed wrong again.

My grandfather McCracken understood archives. He was a classicist and theologian who translated St. Augustine's *City of God* for the Loeb Library. Later in life, his major work was the family genealogy, and what he eventually found out—necessarily obsessive, necessarily incomplete—he published in *The American Genealogist*, a magazine he edited for 20 years.

You might think a genealogist, especially an academic, like my grandfather, would remain invisible in his family history. But my grandfather doesn't. He talks about his travels, he talks about meeting elderly relatives who give him their best recollections. He complains to the Pennsylvania State Library about a family name that has been "barbarously misspelled." An unfamiliar lady cousin tells him she owns a dish bought by a forebear who had died as a teenage paperboy after a fall on the ice, but does "not even offer to show it to me." When his grandfather died, my own grandfather writes that, at two-and-a-half and forbidden to attend the funeral, he went with his parents to his grandparents' house:

... not finding my grandmother, I climbed the very steep stairs and found her crying in a bedroom and comforted her. In the darkened parlor was the great mystery.

Look, here are relatives I've never met, but just-like-that love: Old Bob McCracken the Poet, who converted to Mormonism and was baptized through a hole in the ice on a river, "which brutality disgusted his son." ("Our Robert must have been quite a character," my grandfather writes.) Aunt Phoebe Pickersgill, the caustic wit, "read every word which Samuel Johnson, LLD, had written in English." Our earliest documented antecedent, Thomas McCracken, became senile and was described by an in-law as "a good deal shattered." I love the language of genealogy: *doubtful son, probable wife.*

"We McCrackens sometimes do bizarre things!" Grandpa writes. Yes, and thanks.

There are two plot lines in the genealogy, both precious: the story of how the shattered Thomas McCracken leads to me, and the story of my grandfather driving across country, from the Mormon libraries in Salt Lake City to the courthouses of Pennsylvania to the front porches of distant cousins, trying to figure it all out. Genealogy is equal parts the good stories you hear and the documentation that backs it up; neither is any good alone. For my classicist grandfather—who was also, during World War II, a government cryptologist—the work was endless: How does one group of people lead to another group of people? What documents can be trusted? What can't? Guessing's no good. "If only some kind soul would find a Bible with a complete list of Hugh's children!" my grandfather writes. "I should much prefer that to a pot of gold."

Our work is similar. We're both trying to make sense of the way families fit together. We both want to make that good story true. My grandfather wonders whether his great-grandfather was illegitimate, or rather the son of double first cousins. I have the luxury of

saying: you, fat grandmother who died in a chair, are now the grandmother of someone you never met. You, boy preacher who died at
a young age, now belong to the old woman who wrote letters to
dead relatives, never mind that in real life you weren't related at all.
Now you are.

Come here, Our Robert. I have plans for you.

My grandmother Jacobson was a wonderful and complex
woman, an attorney and small businessperson who died at home
at the age of ninety, the recipient of many letters in my collection
and the author of almost none. The pieces of paper I have from
her don't conjure her up at all. Her diary (which I don't own but
have read) is a very careful record of daily events, nothing more.
She doesn't detail worries or doubts, and the fact is she was a worried and somewhat doubtful person. I think she knew that we'd
read it, eventually, and didn't want to tell us in her diary anything
she hadn't told us already.

One piece of paper I do have: a green Post-it note from late in
her life, which she used to mark a recipe in *The Jewish Cookbook*. It
says:

coffee
bananas
bread
milk
wax beans?

and then, in the corner, written diagonally and underlined,

lottery ticket.

I know that this dates to a time when she was both worried
about money and had become very serious about luck. I don't
know how superstitious she'd previously been, but about two
years before she died, she began to see luck, good and bad, in

everything: She read her horoscope, her children's horoscope, the horoscope of everyone who might touch her life that day. She believed in fortune cookies. She told her own fortune playing solitaire. And she bought lottery tickets, not so much because she believed she might win but because not playing meant she did not believe that sudden good things could happen. She was a businessperson, after all: she knew what a bad investment that weekly dollar was.

It's that moment that makes me want to write fiction, the moment that a person—a person I've known from stories written down or told, or from repeated real-life meetings—is suddenly complicated. Martha, the devoted help, wanted to be more but couldn't manage it. My grandfather, the serious academic, stood in a hallway and longed to see a family relic but couldn't bring himself to ask. My grandmother, the businesswoman, wanted to forget not to gamble, and so wrote herself a note. I itch for more information, and so I make it up, and so I scratch my itch.

I love that little green piece of paper. I keep it taped to my computer monitor. Desideratum to me, though less than ephemera to anyone else.

I could tell dozens of other stories from the pages of family papers: my aunt Blanche's pell-mell record of taking care of her favorite sister, Elizabeth, who was dying of Alzheimer's; Blanche eventually developed that disease herself, and you can see the earliest signs in her notes. (My favorite line: "Dogs are loyal. They are so loyal they will play tricks on you.") My great-uncle David writing from an undisclosed location in Europe during WWII, declaring that he has met a wonderful woman, and he couldn't wait for the family to meet her; she turned out to be my great-aunt Jessica, and they have been married for more than 50 years. My first cousin twice-removed Sarah Werblowsky (1891–1988) kept a faithful diary as a young piano teacher in Des Moines (she wrote as an older person only annually or worse), and she saw Sarah

Bernhardt in Rostand's *The Eaglet* at a downtown vaudeville house but wasn't very impressed. The Divine Sarah in Des Moines, Iowa. I can't tell you how happy I am to know this, or how quickly I tried to work it into fiction.

I have written fiction in some small way about Martha, and Cousins Sarah and Elizabeth; about my grandmother and all her brothers and sisters; about the store that belonged to one set of grandparents and the book-filled house that belonged to the other. The first glimmer of nearly everything I've ever written comes from some scrap of a family story. I have enough material to keep on forever. After all, an archive needs to be organized somehow. Fiction is an unorthodox classification system, but I can't give it up.

That's why I can't write about my own childhood: I can't see around myself. I didn't even keep a diary. There I am, a mostly good-natured kid, whose inner life consists of Spaghettios and wanting to pal around with her older brother, who generally lets her. What's the rest of the story? The rest of the story's dull and delightful. No material here, folks, move along, move along.

The unexamined life may not be worth living, but still I go on.

Not, of course, that what I write is devoid of autobiography. Over the years, for good or ill, I have acquired an inner life. Writing fiction is like calling up a radio psychologist and saying, "Doctor? I have this friend, with this problem." *Tell the truth, now.* "Okay, it's my mother. *She* has a problem. Don't be so nosy or I'll hang up."

Here's a last story. My father's parents were, when I knew them, quiet people. I know now that my version of them is different from anyone else's, but they were my grandparents and I never questioned who I understood them to be. After their deaths, I inherited a cherry chest-of-drawers from their bedroom. I owned this imposing piece of furniture for a few years before I lifted some paper lining from one of the drawers and found a letter.

Part of a letter, actually, written by my grandfather to my grandmother before their marriage.

It was one of the most beautiful love letters I've ever read, full of delight for her person and for their love together. It was passionate and thrilled and almost disbelieving of his great fortune, to have found her. I never imagined my grandfather, my quiet careful grandfather, was the sort of man who'd write any kind of love letter, never mind this kind. Wrong again. And my grandmother had saved it for more than fifty years. I wondered whether she took it out and reread it from time to time, or whether she'd forgotten where she'd put it.

My parents were out of town that weekend, and as it happened I'd agreed to pick them up at the airport. I brought the letter to give to my father—if it meant that much to me, I couldn't imagine what it would mean to him. And so, sitting on a bench near baggage claim, I presented it. "Look what I found," I said.

"Oh," he said, perfectly pleased but not surprised. "Another letter. I'll put it with the others."

Turns out there were many more—my grandparents had written each other several times a day during their courtship. Which makes it, of course, a happier story.

My question is: was that letter more a desideratum for me, or my father? He had the collection, I didn't. Sometimes I regret giving it to him. I've forgotten the exact words my grandfather used, but it doesn't seem right to ask for someone else's love letter back. Someday I'll see it again, I know. Meanwhile, I need it and desire it. I need and desire everything that belongs to my family, and in some ways, I think, that's what I do with my days, writing fiction. I am writing love letters to diaries and Post-it notes and telegrams and birthday cards. I am writing love letters to love letters.

MARILYNNE ROBINSON

Diminished Creatures

Writers have to think. That verb, *think*, is not pretty. It has none of the romance elegance of pensiveness or reflection or contemplation. One plain syllable with a thorn in it, it has come down to us from Norse and Old High German, unphilosophic languages to say the least. Thinking sounds like work, just as it ought to. The word has a way of reminding us that the roots of the brain reach to the tips of the fingers and the soles of the feet, that we see and hear with the brain, that every sense and sensation retrieves for the brain the kind of thing the brain can know. Consciousness is profoundly physical, and physicality is a mental construct. We think with our whole being, continuously, because that is how we are made.

The old mind-body dichotomy was meant first to favor the mind, the flesh being thought of as a sort of sly, unruly, imperfectly domesticated animal, necessary but far from dependable. The supposed rejection of this model in our century has in fact only inverted it. The body has become protagonist and the mind a fractious servitor, full of fear and deception. But we know that the whole being is engrossed in a conversation with itself, and a negotiation with the world, from which essential distinctions arise, like truth and reality and their degrees and their opposites. When and how do we learn the difference between sleeping and waking? What is the meaning of the realness that is so much the character of dream, and how is it reconfigured to dazzle or oppress us as in waking life it very rarely does? A nightmare startles us with its utter knowledge of anything we dread—how a spider moves; what it is to fall; the poor, imperfect, deeply welcome comforts of evasion and concealment. This is urgent physical knowledge that raises sweat and makes the heart race, and it is, as they say, all in our minds. So when I say writers have to think, I absolutely do not mean that they have to drift off into cerebralism, to pillow-fight with the metaphysicians. I mean they have to be faithful to everything they know, in the way that they know it, through all the nerves that feed the voracious brain.

Writers have to deal also with the strange and complicated fact that we are cultural beings. We have studied Shakespeare, or we have not but certainly intend to, or we have not and by no means intend to, or Shakespeare is simply the farthest thing from our minds. These are differences in the way we think of ourselves, and of other people, which have consequence though they lack substance. Someone who plans to become religious on his deathbed probably considers himself already more religious than his neighbor who views the whole subject with contempt. Though no prophet or apostle would encourage him in this conviction, nevertheless he already avails himself of certain of the comforts of religion, sustaining the sneaking hope of an afterlife, for example. And people who are fairly sure they intend to study Shakespeare no doubt consider themselves somewhat superior to those who have no such intention. This is only to say that we orient ourselves in relation to cultural monuments we may never in fact visit. We inhabit a cultural landscape however passively, and define ourselves in relation to it however unconsciously or even unwillingly.

It is precisely in relation to these "monuments of unaging intellect" (to borrow a phrase clearly meant to be viewed with suspicion), that we do not think. And they are monumental in the degree that they seem only to commemorate Thought, to be stranded in time like Easter Island statues, with no one living able to say how things so massive could have been made and erected. I do not intend this as an attack on the canon, or on the idea that certain works are appropriately viewed as the treasures of whole populations. My objection is to the habit of treating such works as categorically different from anything we ourselves can aspire to. What do we feel in Whitman but the physical exhilaration of consciousness? What do we feel in Dickinson but the physical shock of consciousness? We feel their thinking, in other words. They should help us feel our own.

The fear of thinking and knowing is pervasive in our culture because these most human tentatives are for some reason considered to be less human than real life or real experience. "Real" is being used in a very special sense here, since neither life nor experience can be imagined as occurring only from the neck down. What is actually being described is the compartmentalization of awareness to exclude "ideas," that is, canonized thinking, from our own thinking. Ideas are canonized much more arbitrarily than any other kind of cultural artifact, after which they maintain a sort of magical authority, like mummified ancestors, an authority enhanced by their very difference from life.

Here is an example of a mummified idea, one that both expresses and reinforces our fear of knowing, and which is itself a potent demonstration of the persistence of false and disabling ideas, once they are closed off from light and air. There is a story we tell ourselves, a classic form of a tale that exists in many versions and is very current among us now. It goes this way: Once humankind thought the earth was at the center of a clockwork universe, a thing of crystalline spheres, of planets attended by angels, the whole very finite arrangement a tribute to our own unique significance. Then came Copernicus and Galileo, and suddenly, we are told, we found ourselves marginalized, diminished.

The expulsion from Eden seems a minor setback compared to the consequences that are said to have followed from the breaking of this cobweb, since clearly after the Fall we could still believe in our own centrality, as it were. If this story has any truth in it, then the Inquisition was right, and Galileo, merely correct. The Ptolemaic universe, though it was purely imaginary, was nevertheless the firmament we were meant to inhabit, and actual creation a giddy void that stripped us of our dignity and certainty and our peace.

This story is not plausible. The geocentric Middle Ages were violent and harrowing in a degree that argues against their enjoying a special wealth of human self- and mutual esteem. I have read that the ratio of damned to saved in the reckoning of the period could run as high as a hundred-thousand to one, which is only to say that certainty can have great terrors, and that doubt may sometimes come as solace and relief. And the truly pious must have been inclined to prefer God's creation to man's invention, even if we grant Ptolemy's cosmos all the satisfactions that are ascribed to it. The moral of the tale of the loss of the geocentric universe is that reality is not friendly to human self-love. The human passion for knowledge means only that we will know the truth, and the truth will make us small. Then everything good attributed to human culture and experience under what, we are told, were the best circumstances, was in fact illusory. We must have a very dismal view of humankind and of creation, too, if we can accept this.

The irony is that science has created a new geocentricity, much more splendid than Ptolemy's. Our little earth, trapped in the terms of its own understanding, has learned to fashion its limitations into supple nets and to draw very many wondrous things out of this vertiginous sea, most notably the astounding narrative of cosmic origins. Looking outward from our thinking stone we look back in time, because we cannot see distant things as they are in themselves, only as they were when they shed the ancient light that is all we can know of them. Surely there is a deep parable in the fact that we can know only the past, or to put it another way, that the past is there for us to know, preserved to the very life by the limits of our perception. By our nature we make the cosmos a memory of itself, a myth of its own origins, a great divulging. Absent such perceivers it would be none of these things.

Account for all this as one will, a great question remains untouched: What could be more beautiful? What more profound transformation of limitation into vision is to be imagined than this great unscrolling of the heavens to show us extremest antiquity ciphered in light? It is a pure artifact of our insignificance as an object in space. The overwhelming reaches of distance around us are all that could have preserved this oldest narrative for us. One need not begin from, or end in, any kind of theosophical speculation to feel that the place of humankind in such a universe is exalted. If the cosmos is not addressed to us, it is as if it were addressed to us, and that is good enough. Because we are the perceivers, it is a narrative, and it is even now in the course of answering our most ancient questions, for all the world as if we were there to see its vast beginnings with our own eyes.

As a writer I wish to try the effect of believing that my experience is not diminished by the shocks of history, not even true shocks, of which there have been so many that we need not contrive others. There is no before and after in these matters. Life has always made exorbitant demands on human courage. To have a proper respect for the past as well as the present, and to react with poise and dignity to the demands that are made on our own courage, we must bear this fact in mind. As a writer I wish to take into account what is simply true, that the reality science describes, whether macrocosm or microcosm, is elegant, exuberant, fantastical, virtuosic. If necessity can be said to govern it, it is necessity manifest in an effusion of unimaginable possibility. Clearly we have been wrong to imagine the slightest constraint implied by either the word *necessary* or the word *possible*.

But does not this universe, however beautiful, overwhelm us? How can terms be established that will permit the subject of meaning even to be approached? Say that our world is the only pearl in a shoreless sea. If it is a true singularity, if it exists relative to nothing, then how is it to be valued? Is it without value, or is it beyond price? Its purest iridescence is surely that within the luminous calm of its atmosphere, over centuries and generations, questions as to its nature have been asked and answered, truth has been sought and found. It neither explains away the heroism of this fact, nor makes it any whit less astonishing, to say that it is the work of the chemistries of our brains. Why should there be such chemistries, such brains? I have no more practical need than my dog has to know about the fountain of antimatter that pours from the center of our galaxy. And how can I claim to "know" what I cannot imagine? Yet when I read about such things, I feel sharply the privilege of being human.

If one were to generalize about the nature of being, one might reasonably extrapolate from the kind of being that is typical of the universe insofar as it is accessible to our understanding. Void and dark matter would account for vastly the greater part of it, and after that those spectacular manifestations of the extremes of physics-denominated galaxies and stars, with all the phenomena that attend them. The earth is wet and tender as an eye, and so we forget that there are stars orbiting the black hole at the center of our galaxy at nine-hundred miles per second. We are familiar with the fact that in this universe the generality of marvels are of the harrowing kind, and still we think as if there were something ordinary, humdrum, about all this sleeping and waking, sprouting and going to seed, about all the sweet constancies and predictabilities that allow us to hope and love and remember, to hate and cheat and steal, and most essentially and amazingly, to talk about these things to one another. We think of our species as existing in surplus, and to regard our fellows, in the abstract, at least, as a nuisance if not a threat. It is useful to remember that if the universe were portioned out among us the way planets were once thought to be put in the care of angels, each one of us would have charge of more stars than we see on a clear night, of more space than the whole universe was thought to contain only decades ago. However, we may crowd our little habitat, we are rare even to vanishing in cosmic terms. And yet, in this calm province, under this mild moon, I can report that my dog loves me, though not without reservation. What could be more unaccountable? We while away time in our little ark of world, nothing and everything, while the wild floods of being roar around us. It is an old tale and a very pretty one.

Very well. But what does all this mean when it comes to putting words on paper? It means, first of all, that we may not think of ourselves as diminished creatures, less at home in the world than people were in any other age. We can only be truly and inalienably native to it—as Genesis points out, we are made of it. Our intelligence is remarkable in kind, but single-cell animals can eat and reproduce, and they can communicate and organize and collaborate, and they can deploy truly remarkable strategies of attack and defense, as we are now learning to our sorrow. These brainless creatures behave in a way we do not hesitate to call intelligent when we see it in our own kind (putting aside for the moment the fact that we are also made of *them*). This is only to say that there is no more dichotomy between ourselves and the living world than there is between the mind and the body. The fact that this needs to be said points up what may be the great human mystery, after all— our capacity for error and falsification, which is so overriding as to make foolishness of our intelligence, to our own great grief and peril and impoverishment. Good fiction is not false. It is a complex and figurative statement of an intuition of truth. By truth I may mean nothing more than a commerce between the mind and the world in which there is alert and lively respect for both parties to the transaction. If we could know as feeling what we can know as fact, our literature would be transformed—into something very like the best in all the books we have always loved.

JAMES HYNES

Why I Bother

All writers are vain, selfish and lazy, and at the very bottom of their motives there lies a mystery. Writing a book is a horrible, exhausting struggle, like a long bout of some painful illness. One would never undertake such a thing if one were not driven on by some demon whom one can neither resist nor understand.

—*George Orwell, "Why I Write"*

The lives of fiction writers have never been easy, and because we don't have any choice in the matter, we try to make this difficulty into a matter of pride. We pitch this necessary self-aggrandizement in all sorts of ways. Sometimes we make it into a noble struggle against the world's indifference, or even a crusade against the world's effort to repress literature or bury it under a mountain of trash; William Faulkner's or Toni Morrison's grandiloquent Nobel Prize speeches come to mind. More often, in recent years, as the culture becomes more ironic around us, we often spin the struggle as something darkly romantic and even perverse, the writing of fiction as a particularly skillful and entertaining hustle, with the writer as a beautiful but two-timing film noir Medusa, willing to spill the secrets of friends and loved ones. "Writers," said Joan Didion, as heartless as Barbara Stanwyck or Ava Gardner, "are always selling someone out."

These varieties of dissembling mask, as they're meant to, a real dilemma, namely, why write? Every writer faces this question, usually daily, as in, why write today?—and less often (one hopes) in the middle of the night, as in, why write at all? These are the opposite ends of a very slippery sliding scale, as "I'm too tired to write today" elides with frightening ease into "I'm too tired to carry on with this." In between are all the reasons writers give up writing, for a week, for a year, forever: I'm in debt and I need to get a job. Nobody buys my books. My books don't stay in print. Nobody will publish me anymore. I drink too much, I have writer's block, there's more money in journalism or screenplays. I can't get tenure, or now that I have tenure, why break a sweat? I'm finally so happy that I don't need the catharsis of writing, or I'm still so unhappy that I need catharsis too much to concentrate.

All of these are personal excuses, and an indifferent world provides a long list of more objective and frighteningly rational reasons not to write prose fiction: the dominance of film, television, pop music, and the Net, which soak up the lion's share of money and recognition in our culture; the increasingly corporate centralization of publishing and bookselling; the diminishing market in academic positions for artists, coupled with an increasing number of MFA programs full to bursting, like seed pods, with young, ambitious writers.

I could go on, but it boils down to this: There are too many of us, and too many of us are unnecessary. An individual writer may rise above the pack from time to time, but on the whole we are easily replaceable. Only actors or other performers endure worse rejection, because they often have it spoken to their faces—you're too old, you're too young, you're too fat—while writers have the thin mediation of the rejection letter. But rejection at arm's length is still rejection. To support our work, most fiction writers inhabit the more menial and less glamorous regions of the literary economy. Usually there is a cubicle involved. Without us, there would be fewer tech writers, copyeditors, bookstore clerks, composition teachers, or junior professors. There would be fewer people to write book reviews, marketing copy, software manuals, reference books, *Penthouse* captions ("My name is Bree ... do you want to play?"), grammar workbooks, or in-flight magazine articles. We are the migrant laborers of publishing, willing to take the jobs that nobody else wants, for something less than a living wage.

Finally, there remains our own unique existential burden, what Orwell calls the "horrible, exhausting struggle" of writing itself. Most of us don't really understand when we're young what a spiritual, emotional, and even physical toll writing a book takes on a person. We lose sleep, we run our nerves ragged with anxiety, we abuse the patience of loved ones; we live on wild expectations of success and then learn to be grateful we are published at all; we doubt our own talent and even our sanity for long periods of time. Just writing this essay is probably as bad for me as a pack of cigarettes.

I'm laying all this on thick in order to get at an aspect of the writer's life that doesn't often get addressed in essays of this sort. In the face of rejection, indifference, and outright humiliation, why does anyone bother to write prose fiction? And, having done it for a while with indifferent success or no success at all, why does anyone carry on?

One of the more famous answers to this question is George Orwell's essay "Why I Write." I read this essay at an impressionable age for a writer, in my mid-twenties, and for a long time I adopted Orwell's four reasons as my own. Orwell faced a different set of circumstances, but the four reasons he gives struck me as fundamental at the time:

1. Sheer egoism ("Desire to seem clever, to be talked about, to be remembered after death, to get your own back on grown-ups who snubbed you in childhood, etc., etc.");

2.   Aesthetic enthusiasm ("Perception of beauty in the external world, or, on the other hand, in words and their right arrangement");

3.   Historical impulse ("Desire to see things as they are, to find
out true facts and store them up for the use of posterity"); and

4.   Political purpose ("Desire to push the world in a certain
direction, to alter other people's idea of the kind of society that
they should strive after").

When I was in my twenties, the last of these loomed largest; I
wanted to write political fiction and tough little essays on pop culture in the style of Orwell. In my early middle age that motivation
has faded almost entirely away, partly because my left-liberal politics seem downright quaint after the end of the Cold War, but
mostly because age and cynicism have eroded the utopian
impulse in me, an impulse any left-liberal needs to go on. Orwell's
third reason, to record history, to get the facts straight, has likewise lost some of its importance. People still write about history
and current events, but the recording of facts has been largely
taken over by audiovisual media. The handful of great novels
about World War II and Vietnam notwithstanding (to take an
obvious example), those wars exist in the larger public consciousness exclusively as images from film and video documentaries, or
as the glossier representations of Hollywood, from John Wayne
to Tom Hanks.

Sheer egoism and aesthetic pleasure, on the other hand, are
beyond refutation. In fact, in the years since I first read "Why I
Write," I've come to realize that these two reasons, with variations, constitute all the reasons I continue to write. I offer the following with the understanding that these motivations are personal to me, and that even those that might apply to other writers
may not apply to all of them, and that none of them may apply to

anybody fifty years from now. In the meantime, here is one struggling writer's rosary for the turn of the century:

1. Sheer egoism, of course, though I prefer to call it "lust for money, power, and fame." No writer can function without ambition; it's the hot little engine at the heart of all art and literature. But it is as dangerous as it is necessary, and it has never been more dangerous to the spirit and good intentions of the writer than it is in our time. The simple egoism that any artist in any age needs has been amplified by a culture that worships success, money, and celebrity more than anything else. Young writers, and even not so young ones, are marinated in this culture, and we foolishly tend to judge our success not only against best-selling authors, which is futile enough, but against successful filmmakers or pop singers. This is madness, for a couple of reasons.

One is that writers of fiction hardly ever achieve the level of fame that our culture celebrates. Apart from a handful of household names, even the most notorious literary author doesn't have a readership that matches the weekly numbers of a low-rated sitcom. Schedule appearances by Jay McInerney and Jerry Seinfeld at opposite ends of a shopping mall, and watch which way the crowd goes.

The second reason is that winning fame is almost entirely a function of luck. Every writer, whether he means to or not, plays the zeitgeist like a slot machine, and for every literary writer who hits the jackpot, there are thousands more who walk away with emptied pockets. Even lowering our sights and aiming for the public's taste is no guarantee of success: For every Tom Clancy, there are probably hundreds of former insurance salesmen writing techno-thrillers for angry white men, and most of them never even make it into print. Those of us who are less successful often console ourselves over the difficulty of writing by saying jauntily, hey, if it weren't hard, any idiot could do it. But a glance at the bestseller list will tell you than a lot of idiots do, very successfully.

The point is a simple one: Fame is the spur, but the desire for it can scorch or ruin a life.

2.   Intellectual curiosity and/or curiosity about my own life. This is similar to Orwell's "historical impulse," but my version doesn't require, as Orwell's seems to, that the writer know "true facts" and "things as they are." As I said above, this function is fulfilled for the public nowadays mostly by film, television, and the Internet. My version is a little more postmodern and less public: I write about a subject in order to explain it to myself. A novel is my way of thinking out loud. This was the case with my first published novel, which was about the contemporary troubles in Northern Ireland. The best way—the only way, in fact—for me to make sense of the complicated history and shifting battle lines of Ulster was to create a story about it, to put characters inside the situation and see what happened. I never intended it to serve as a history of the Troubles, but I hope that my novel reveals certain universal truths about love, political commitment, and loyalty more vividly than any nonfiction account could.

A novel does not have to be about a large public subject to serve this purpose; a family or a relationship between two people is enough to fill a book. That is why I include curiosity about oneself: Every work of fiction, whether it is overtly autobiographical or not, has its autobiographical elements. Every writer is working out something personal in a narrative, even if the only personally revealing element is the author's choice of subject matter. Even when we don't think we're doing it, we are. I published a novella whose main character, a failing academic, was consciously intended to be a conniving, lying, cheating, vain, careerist little asshole, whose only redeeming characteristic was a certain nasty wit. It took an ex-girlfriend of mine to mention, with seeming offhandedness, that certain aspects of this jerk reminded her of me. (I mentioned this to my current love and she only smiled.)

So whether a writer intends to recreate his own life in his fiction or not, he is liable to learn something new about himself, and not necessarily what he wanted to hear. The danger of this motivation is that the writer merely engages in narcissism or wish-fulfillment. Wish-fulfillment is the heart of most popular fiction, but literary fiction is far from exempt. The current bull market for no-holds-barred memoir aside *(I Fucked J.D. Salinger*, or whatever it was called), there are plenty of literary novels where nicer, funnier, better-looking versions of the author get their own back, as Orwell put it, and have great sex along the way.

3.   To reproduce the experience of reading my favorite books. This motivation is quite conscious on my part. My first novel was written to explain Northern Ireland to myself, but to do so I deliberately modeled the story on books by authors who mean a great deal to me, specifically, Joseph Conrad, Graham Greene, John Le Carre, and Robert Stone. In fact, it's a toss-up as to what was more important to me: the desire to figure out the Troubles, or the desire to rewrite *Dog Soldiers* and *The Secret Agent*. This impulse may be fundamental to literature: Flaubert and Stendahl begat Conrad, Conrad and John Buchan begat Greene, and so on. This imitative impulse is the first sign of wanting to be a writer, the feeling a young artist gets after finishing a really good book that makes him or her say "I could do that." The danger is that one never grows beyond imitation; commercial literature is full of imitations of Tolkien, Stephen King, Anne Rice, et al. Again, literary fiction is not exempt: The sobriquet "the new Cheever" is often just a lazy reviewer's shorthand, but sometimes it's true. Unoriginality is not exclusive to pop fiction.

4.   To erase myself in the creative act. Writers are achingly self-conscious people, whose live-wire awareness of everything around them, or of the constant engine-room hum of their own imaginations, makes them crave some sort of peace. And the ironic heart of the matter is that most writers get this peace from

the act of creation itself. The paradigm for this is addiction. If you follow the career of a writer, from the credulous young reader utterly lost in someone else's story to the trembling, chain-smoking insomniac trying to create his own, it's the classic progression from the first harmless toke to the spike in the arm.

This motivation is closely tied to the previous one. The desire to recreate *The Secret Agent* by writing my own book is not just a desire to write as well as Joseph Conrad; it is a desire to recreate the same pleasure I felt when reading it, a pleasure that took me completely out of my own experience, and even out of my own self-awareness, and put me in the park around Greenwich Observatory, carrying a bomb in a paint can. This is not the same thing as reading for escape, where the mind just switches off and lets the narrative play as if upon a screen. Rather, it is an experience in which I fully inhabit another world, where my mind is fully engaged—but not as myself.

Another way to put it is to say that the most sublime experience in writing comes when the writer feels as if he is *remembering* the book, not creating it. It is as if the book is Out There someplace, and the writer is simply recording what he has heard. This is what a writer means when he says, after multiple, agonizing drafts, "this is it," the relief that what's on the page at last matches the melody only the writer can hear.

This relief is certainly not unique to me; all varieties of writer talk about this element of unconscious release at the heart of writing. Much of William Gaddis's novel *The Recognitions* is devoted to it, and in a recent article, Stephen King talks about "the boys in the basement" who write his books. In the same article, King quotes Maxwell Perkins referring to Thomas Wolfe as a wind chime: "The wind blew through him and he just rattled." This smacks of all sorts of things—of vulgar Platonism, of New Age channeling—which makes it hard to explain, let alone justify, but I don't know how else to say it: The most vivid and profoundly spiritual moments of my life, the moments when I completely forget where and who I am, come when I am writing fiction.

But (you might say) isn't this just imitation writ large? Isn't that perfect Platonic ideal of a book I'm trying to reproduce just somebody else's book, dimly remembered? And doesn't this conception of creativity take away agency? Perhaps. There's a very clever short story by a long-forgotten *New Yorker* writer named Russell Maloney called "Inflexible Logic," in which a wealthy eccentric decides to test the old cliché about a monkey and a typewriter. He puts six chimpanzees, six typewriters, and an endless supply of typing paper in his conservatory, and immediately the chimps start recreating, "word for word and comma for comma," the entire canon of English literature. Finally, a friend of the wealthy eccentric, a mathematician, is driven insane by the fact that the monkeys don't produce a single page of gibberish (which statistics says they should—reams of it, in fact), and he shoots all the chimpanzees. That mathematician could just as well have been a writer maddened by the secret suspicion we all harbor that the book we sweated over for months or years could just as well have been written by our cat.

But there's another, profounder story that gets at the heart of the matter, Jorge Luis Borges' "Pierre Menard, Author of the *Quixote*," a fictional essay about an author who sets out to write *Don Quixote*—not "another *Don Quixote*," writes Borges, "which would be easy, but *the Don Quixote.*" Menard does not intend to transcribe the book (though, according to Borges, there's no way to prove he did not), nor does he intend to try to recreate the consciousness or circumstances of the seventeenth century. Rather, he intends to create *Don Quixote* from a twentieth-century consciousness, which means that it would be a completely new book, utterly different from Cervantes' version, and maybe even better.

This is a classically Borgesian metaphysical parlor trick, hilarious and mind-boggling all at once. Hilarious, as when Borges quotes a passage from Cervantes and calls it "a mere rhetorical praise of history," and then quotes the same passage (word for word and comma for comma the same) from Menard and calls it "astounding," since it comes from a twentieth-century writer who reached the same conclusion as a seventeenth-century one. Mind-boggling, because Borges is right, finally—Pierre Menard's achievement is a different one than Cervantes'. The fact that it's the *same book* is finally irrelevant; it was the struggle to write it that counts.

I know how crazy this sounds, but I can't think of a better way to express the feeling I get when I am writing. I can't even say for sure that the writing that results from this spiritual release is even my best work. I only know that the pleasure I take in it is so similar to the pleasure I take from reading someone else's best work as to be identical, and I can only conclude that the two pleasures come from the same place, which brings me full circle back to the original question and threatens to unravel the tapestry of answers I've stitched together. If I get the same pleasure from reading as from creation, why endure rejection, bad nerves, the world's indifference, and all the rest? Why write at all? As Borges says in "Pierre Menard," "There is no exercise of the intellect which is not, in the final analysis, futile."

Maybe all literary achievement comes from sheer egoism; maybe I write my own work because there is more pleasure to be derived from erasing myself than from letting someone else do it. Perhaps each writer is his or her own ouroburos, eagerly opening our egos wide in order to devour our egos, and vanishing in a little flash of creation that leaves a story or a poem or a book behind. Whatever it is, this mysterious alchemy of self-effacement and self-aggrandizement is what keeps me coming back to writing, no matter what my success or failure in the world. Since I've come full circle, I'll return to Orwell:

For all one knows that demon [that makes one write] is simply the same instinct that makes a baby squall for atten-

tion. And yet it is also true that one can write nothing readable unless one constantly struggles to efface one's own personality. Good prose is like a window pane. I cannot say with certainty which of my motives are the strongest, but I know which of them deserve to be followed.

I can't speak for anyone else, but that's good enough for me.

SCOTT SPENCER

The Difference Between Being Good and Being a Good Writer

When I taught writing recently, I sometimes went out for drinks and dinner with my students. They were witty, good-hearted, and generally a wonderfully polite group of men and women in their twenties. There was an absence of shouting, confrontation, accusation, proclamation, drunkenness, tears, outrageous costume, glaring idiosyncrasy, or any other kinds of acting out that normally makes for wonderful anecdotes later on. At the various pubs or pizza parlors we frequented, we could have been a group of people from the history or geology department.

A lot of what made them so personable could only be the result of their having been well brought up, and if they had not actually read Flaubert's advice to writers—live like a bourgeois and save your madness for Art—they were behaving as if they had. But they were also feeling the undeniable pressure to conform exerted by the group. A bunch of young football players exerts its own species of tyranny about manliness and fearlessness, a crew of young seminarians watches one another for signs of spiritual laxness, and, I'm afraid, a class of beginning writers, who must read and criticize one another's efforts, develops an unspoken sense that a well-made story filled with familiar ironies is much less likely to make you look like a fool in the stark light of the workshop than any foray into stylistic risk or personal revelation. Today, the young writer is often writing something that she knows her classmates are going to read next week. And after they read it they are all going to talk to her about it. In front of the teacher. The archetype of the monomaniacal unknown writer, alone in a garret with no audience but The Muse, has given way to the young scholar whose fledgling steps must be made in full view not only of professional writers but sharp-tongued peers, with whom, by the very nature of the academic system, they feel in competition.

And so the new crop of writers coming up through the workshop system tend to be outwardly somewhat conservative. Some of this is because we are living in a conservative cultural climate, which affects everyone. There's not an awful lot a writing teacher can do about that. But some of the conservatism is a function of fear—sheer terror, really—and there are things a teacher can do about *that*. A friend of mine advised me to bring a lot of candy to each class, and that seemed to have had a good effect. Countering the gladiatorial atmosphere of the workshop with *excesses* of openness and permissiveness is also something worth trying. Most importantly of all, we should encourage everyone—including ourselves—to get free of that cornerstone of socialization that tells us Under No Circumstance Shall You Make a Fool of Yourself.

It's usually a good idea to avoid making a fool of yourself, or opening yourself up to ridicule. People in positions of authority like cops or congressmen actively dread being made to look foolish. Average citizens and mediocre writers try to avoid having so much as an eyebrow arched in their direction, and quite often succeed. Essayists in *Time* magazine, for example, manage to sound witty and self-possessed, no matter what they are writing about. Commercial fiction, sure of its mission, lulled to stylistic sleep by its assumptions about its audience, might be laughable to some, but the writers of those works run little risk of feeling foolish because most often the criticisms come from beyond the arc of the work's intentions. Earnest writers who write with a clear political or social or (God help us) religious agenda might be mocked by those who don't agree with them, but again, their target audience (that is, people who have agreed with them for *years)* will not find them remotely foolish. They will find them sincere; they will find them correct.

But how can we create real literature without making ourselves vulnerable to mockery? It is, after all, not only the work itself that is open to devastating criticism, but critics and academics and rank-and-file readers can treat us as if we were the village idiot or transgressors against moral decency, or as if we were vulgar, uncouth, or even uncool. There is a level of personal risk in writing, and like other risks, the return is not assured. Before he was acknowledged as a genius, James Joyce had to risk being known as a purveyor of gibberish. Vladimir Nabokov was willing to have members of the Cornell faculty wonder just how much Humbert was in him, willing even for neighbors to call their daughters into the house when the suddenly suspect professor Nabokov emerged from his house in khaki shorts and a safari shirt, sporting a butterfly net. There are still people, one can surmise, who would feel a little queasy leaving the distinguished and erudite Philip Roth alone in the kitchen with a pound of uncooked liver.

Not behaving like a fool requires a certain level of repression, a steady inner vigilance, and a willingness to let what used to be called the superego take charge of certain situations, especially if the situations themselves are charged. Literature, however, thrives on an abandonment of repression, a willingness to say anything, espouse, describe, and suggest anything at all. In life, our most frightening, bewildering, suggestive scenarios about our bodies, our loved ones, about space, time, mortality, and retribution are relegated to dreams, when our superego has fallen into a stupor, and all that we have left unexpressed can present itself in a kind of carnival of jesters and ghouls. Writing is a way of dreaming out loud, and in public; even the most noble tales, if truly told, contain within them nuggets of evidence about the teller: soft spots, blind spots, wounds, weird obsessions. Wariness about these potentially embarrassing aspects and a willingness to weed them out is a deadly practice for a writer.

Vigilance about wounding or angering people who might recognize themselves in our work can also be a cold dead hand on our work. The way I see it, when we ask the society at large to take us seriously as writers, we are also in effect promising that we will take our job as society's wide-awake dreamers and recording secretaries seriously. We are being paid (or, more often, we are asking to be paid) for *saying* things, not for *not* saying things. A writer who will not risk hurting someone's feelings is finally no more effective than a firefighter who will not smash in windows.

Tact is wonderful in a friend, and an ability to carry secrets with you into the grave is surely worthy of our admiration. But I can't think of any writer who is read for his or her tact. So, let's not take any vows never to divulge family secrets. If you're worried about being cut out of a will, you should just wait for your inheritance and then start writing. With the sudden prominence of the memoir and the personal essay, a certain tell-all mentality has become somewhat fashionable, but what has become even more fashionable is criticizing the tell-all mentality. Writing about your husband's repulsive nighttime habits or your mother's annihilating vanity might not, in the end, make very interesting reading for those not in your immediate circle, but an inability to ever express the most strange, scandalous, and upsetting things you know will make writing like cooking before Prometheus.

If we're going to ask someone to take the time to read what we've written, there is a promise on our part implicit in the transaction, a pledge that we're finally willing to risk everything— peace of mind, reputation—to repay the commitment they are making to our work. In order to make good on that commitment, we need to be fearless, unsparing, and just a little bit feverish.

In life, a certain degree of conformity is wise, humble, and it also saves a lot of time. (Who needs to spend a minute deciding what to wear to a funeral?) In writing, however, the less conformity the better—except, perhaps, when it comes to spelling and punctuation. Literature welcomes the offbeat, the unreasonable, the furious, the wounded, the salacious. Literature believes in talking dogs, in love worth dying for, ghosts, and Grand Inquisitors. If what we believe in is the measured response, a balanced diet and plenty of rest, keeping our deepest fears to ourselves, and not being the one left standing when ten people are scrambling to sit in the nine remaining chairs, then we must recognize these impulses for what they are—guides to a happy life, but detriments to writing.

JAMES ALAN McPHERSON

Workshopping Lucius Mummius

*"'As for the shows,' said objectors, 'let them continue in the old
Roman way, whenever it falls to the praetors to celebrate them, and provided that no citizen is obliged to compete. Traditional morals, already
gradually deteriorating, have been utterly ruined by this imported lax-
ity!' ... Two hundred years have passed since the Triumph of Lucius
Mummius—who first gave that sort of show here—and during that
time no upper class Roman has ever demeaned himself by professional
acting ..."*

—Tacitus, *Annals of Imperial Rome*

I

I lived last year in a townhouse behind the private gate of an
upper-class community in Los Altos, California. Although there
was no official gate, a sign posted on an arch at the entrance
warned that only residents and their guests were entitled to drive
up the private road leading to the townhouses. I spent my nights
secure inside my own rented townhouse several hundred feet
from the protective gate. My days were spent beyond the protec-

tive barricade of another gate, which guarded the very beautiful hilltop quarters of the Center for Advanced Studies in the Behavioral Sciences at Stanford University. Atop this hill were the offices of an assembly of academics from the best universities in the country, as well as from abroad. We met for lunch each day at noon and discussed, during intense conversations, our various projects. My colleagues, who were mostly social scientists, used a highly refined and specialized language. Phrases like *statistical models* and *variations* were employed with the ease of a priestly caste reciting incantations. There was another word that aroused extreme suspicion among the social scientists. The word was *narrative.* This word was intended to evoke the "anecdotal" evidence that was not susceptible to rigorous analysis. This evidence was viewed with suspicion because it was contained in stories that did not have any scientific value. Over the course of nine months, I was able to understand, and to even respect, the scientific rigor that had been evolved to achieve the respectability now enjoyed by the social sciences. But I soon began to miss the emotional muscle, the complexity of feelings, within the "narratives" that were so suspect within the intellectual precincts beyond that particular gate.

Each Thursday at three P.M., inside the private clubhouse of the gated community in Los Altos, I met with a group of elderly people who had begun a writing circle. The idea had originated with Leon Wortman, a retired businessman, who had grown dissatisfied with the quality of exchange among the people in the writing circle sponsored by the Senior Citizen's Center in Palo Alto. Leon had circulated a proposal among the occupants of the townhouses, and soon a small group of elderly people, all of them retired, began to meet. Leon himself was writing a novel based on his exploits as an undercover operative in the OSS during World War II. Ida, another member of the group, had been crippled since birth, had no children, and was trying to recapture the emotional texture of the Jewish immigrant experience in New York. Another woman, a

retired teacher, was reaching back in memory to connect emotionally with the communal life of small towns in Oklahoma, Kansas,
and Texas, where she had grown up and where she had had roots.
Another man, retired from teaching in a prep school in
Washington, DC, was writing, for his sons and daughter, a memoir
about the early years of this century and the high points of his life
with his deceased wife. All of them were looking back toward substance. As a longtime teacher, one with a conditioned hunger for
"workshopping," I tried as best I could to help my neighbors refine
their narratives in ways that would improve their writing styles.
But the greatest pleasure, for me at least, resided in the opportunity to encourage the freedom of narration within a context in
which anecdotal evidence, the emotional texture of the lives people had actually lived, was not suspect.

These contrasting memories of narrative "sites" remained with
me when I returned to my regular teaching duties at the Iowa
Writers' Workshop. I returned to my spacious office in the elegant
Dey House, the new home of the Master in Fine Arts Program, the
Mother of all such programs, to a context in which "narratives" are
still held in high regard. Such is the influence of the Iowa Writers'
Workshop that its graduates now staff most of the other writing
programs in the country. News reports, arriving on almost a
weekly basis, testify to Iowa's great influence. The Art Institute of
Chicago has launched its own writing program, one staffed by
Iowa graduates. The *Writers Chronicle,* the official newspaper of the
Associated Writers Program, lists writing programs from Alabama
to Wyoming, all soliciting applicants, sponsoring workshops, listing names of famous graduates. The fact that there are so many
programs is a testimony to the fact that universities, for both commercial and aesthetic reasons, have made homes for aspiring writers, meeting the need once met by newspapers. The success of
such programs, at least as providers of space for writers, is noted,
even with only wry humor, by John Updike in his recent collection
of stories, *Bech at Bay*:

There are these facts, this happened and that happened, all told in this killingly clean prose. They have advanced degrees in creative writing; they go to these workshops and criticize each other; there is nothing left to criticize, but something is missing. I don't know what it is—a love of the world, some hope beyond the world.

Reading this comment by John Updike reminded me of the disjuncture I had sensed, last year, between the scientific techniques of the social scientists at the Center for Behavioral Studies and the rough but heartfelt prose of the senior citizens in the townhouses of my gated community. The one group of specialists had succeeded in reducing the human complexity of life to statistical models, while the older people were wise enough to still remain in awe of its magical and improvisational nature. The one group focused on surfaces; the other group focused on human essentials based on lived experience. The one group evolved a technology in the sense defined by the Swiss novelist Max Frisch—"the knack of so arranging the world that we don't have to experience it." The other group had already experienced the world and was trying to evolve forms that would make that experience of value, and useful, to others. While I do not agree with Updike's insinuation that workshops help to evolve techniques that tend to substitute for deeply felt emotional realities, I do believe that writing workshops can be influenced by cultural trends that flow into them from the outside world. To the extent that they do, the quality of the fiction written within such sites can be undermined.

Last fall the cultural critic Roger Rosenblatt, in a television review of the film *Saving Private Ryan,* offered his perception of the basic problem:

This art of persuasive appearance is true of the work of an entire generation, who have mastered the trappings of things but not the center. What has happened, I think, not just in movies but in books, theater, architecture, even government, is that technique has replaced meaning. Technique is so polished, so expert, it *becomes* meaning. . . . Many books have a center because there will always be authentic writers.

But too many are made, as if with Lego parts, so much exposition, so much violence, so much sex. Books are acquired, not edited. They come prefabricated and presold. Magazines are made. Name your niche and fill it. Buildings are made to look like buildings. . . . Political candidates are built out of appearance, voice, the ability to deliver one-liners, out of everything except what is inside them. The inside of the candidate, the reason for the person to behave as he or she does, is not considered an element of the product. . . . The best in art and life comes from a center—something urgent and powerful—an ideal or emotion that insists on its being. From that insistence a shape emerges and creates its structure out of passion. If you begin with a structure, you have to make up the passion. And that's very hard to do. . . .

Roger Rosenblatt's critique of the current culture's devotion to technique over meaning raises deeply serious questions. Just how much are the many writing workshops, with their heavy emphasis on technique over passion, contributing to an aesthetic that celebrates the outside, the surface of things, while obscuring the essential inside world, the subjective world, that is essential to good fiction? But much more important, what can writing workshops offer as creative solutions to this entrenched cultural problem?

II

I am imagining that, as a workshop teacher, I have enrolled in my class a descendent of Lucius Mummius, that illustrious

General Lucius Mummius who, during the Third Punic War between Rome and Carthage, had sacked Corinth, the last of the free Greek City States, and had hauled cartload after cartload of sacred relics back to Rome. He received a Triumph for his ostentatious display of loot, believing, along with the mob, that he was now in possession of "culture." He did not know, or even suspect, the relations of the treasures, torn from their ritual basis, to the religious and ethical life of the Greeks who had made them. To Lucius Mummius, they represented only a surface displace of his journey from warrior to *novus*, a "new man" now in possession of refinement and taste. In the reign of the Emperor Nero, the writer Petronius Abiter would write satires about such *novi* as Lucius Mummius and Trimalchio in his *Satyricon*. Many centuries later, the American writer F. Scott Fitzgerald would reexamine the old problem of surfaces obscuring substance in his novel *Trimalchio in West Egg*, later renamed *The Great Gatsby*. But Fitzgerald, the great writer, would have never envisioned the time when most meanings surrounding the writer would be surface meanings, a time in which the passionate subjective voice of Nick Carroway would find no place in fiction.

To help instruct my wealthy student in the true meaning of his cultural artifacts, I would expose him first to a book, *The Death of Adam*, by Marilynne Robinson, who raises this issue in her brilliant essays. She argues for the preeminence of meaning over fact. That is, beyond the fact itself there should exist a fundamental principle grounded in the essentials of human life; a principle with which one can identify, when the identification with the undefinable is complete, a meaning that defines one's own meaning. Ms. Robinson's argument is not just that of a "contrarian." Even the right-wing press, specifically *Chronicles of Culture*, supports Ms. Robinson in her assessment of the current state of things:

As our lives become drabber and less substantial, we become obsessed with celebrities—body-sculpted starlets,

basketball players, and jet-setting politicos. *People* magazine is our Bible and Larry King is the greatest prophet.
Every day, American life becomes less and less like something the authors of the *Federalist* would have understood
and more and more like scenes from Petronius' *Satyricon*,
where sex substitutes for love, profits for productivity.
Petronius lived in the time of the Emperor Nero, when the
Romans no longer voted for their consuls but were content
to worship whatever buffoon had been selected to be the
god-man who ruled the world's only remaining super-
power...."

I would add to my lecture that Daniel J. Boorstin made the
same points in his book, *The Image,* as long ago as 1961. But when
Boorstin wrote, there did not exist then the technological
processes that have now helped to revolutionize the transformation of emotional language into thin images. In Boorstin's time
there still existed, beneath the various surfaces, a core of com-
monly held values that taught what it meant to be human. Now
we are not so sure of this. Issues of multiculturalism and rela-
tivism aside, there seems to be underway a steady retreat from
engagement with these core values. Instead, there is a proud celebration of the image, the polished surface, that is offered without
irony of hesitation, as a *substitute* for the core value. This sea
change has encouraged the development of a new art-speech
grounded in technology: *buzz, spin, image rehabilitation, synergy.*
While such developments were not encouraged by the numerous
workshops, the aesthetic, commercial, and most especially the
technological preoccupations of the world outside the workshops
tend to filter into such specialized enclaves. I recall an incident,
from nearly twelve years ago, when a student came to my home
in tears. He showed me a letter from a senior editor at a prestigious magazine, an editor who had been encouraging the young
writer's work. The editor now informed the writer that his maga-

zine was no longer publishing "minimalist" fiction. I recall attending a lecture, about five years ago, given by an editor at a major
publishing house. She advised the students that publishers were
no longer accepting stories or novels about incest. A comparable
commercial reaction has already been mounted against the memoir form. Then there is the new synergetic operation now managed by Ms. Tina Brown, a literary outlet that will transform stories from magazine-to-book-to-film with the wave of a high-tech
wand. Subjected to the shifting commercial tastes of publishers
and editors, young writers are being encouraged to perform "dog
tricks"—to make radical adjustments in the ways their passions
connect with artificial forms. They can be tempted to please commercial Sirens whose songs may mislead young writers trying to
follow their own passions toward some home port that is familiar
to their own feelings.

This fascination with the surface beauty of things is what
inspired L. Mummius to haul into Rome, in 147 B.C., cart after
cart of the spoils of Corinth. He had no understanding of the aesthetic sensibilities, level of taste, and meaning that had gone into
the creation of these artifacts. Mummius represented the triumph
of a civilization with a technological bias (military, architectural,
roads, arches, camps) that was beginning to be troubled by a void
in its spiritual life. Possession of the artifacts, then, symbolized a
connection with the meaning of the culture that had produced
them. But this assumption of connection and of meaning was left
to those who viewed the artifacts from outside their settled ritual
context. To such perceptions they represented only wealth. But to
the Greeks who made them, they represented a deeply serious
connection to the city-state of Corinth, to the meaning of the
polis, to civic concerns, and ultimately, connections to the Gods.
The Greeks were serious spectators, ever on the lookout for the
ideal, the universal, the perfected form of something great. To
them, beauty was an everyday necessity because the experience of
it led to an appreciation of truth, and an appreciation of truth led

to goodness. Perfectionism, then, was the aesthetic standard. One should never pay attention to the trite, the aesthetically unpleasing, because what one paid attention to could shape one's character. To such sensibilities, art served as a prop for living the highest kind of life. Mummius brought cart after cart of Greek artifacts into Rome. But he had amassed only the surface of the culture from which they had come. He had the material wealth to put on display, but he lacked the inner refinement to actually *look* at it ... to appreciate on the deepest levels of his self the aesthetic ideals the artifacts represented.

Facile analogies to the moral and aesthetic condition of Rome during its decadence are very easy to make, so I should be cautious with my generalizations. I would, nonetheless, like to continue with the idea of the ancient Greek as spectator, because it suggests a somewhat comparable development in American culture, one that exists outside the communities of the workshops but that, like trends in publishing, affects the quality of work done by young writers. It seems to me that the electronic media have now appropriated the word-of-mouth process that has always existed at the basis of storytelling and has transformed it into only another thin surface. It also seems to me that the news media now dramatize in a scene-specific way the deepest and most complex of human feelings, but almost always in a fashion that is emotionally numb. I watch news stories about disasters—earthquakes, fires, bombings, hurricanes, murders. The victims of such disasters, having already been instructed in the limited range of emotional responses required by a sound bite, have learned to script and economize their televised grief-stricken responses. This is for all the other spectators who will be watching them. But their efforts to be brief, instead of conveying a tragic sense, can become comic. One female victim of a tornado, several years ago, gave such an economic and tearful account of her losses that it prompted the on-site television reporter to say, "*Wonderful!*" Then there are the televised stories that are becoming a staple feature on both local and national newscasts. "Everyone has a story to tell," the wandering reporter advises. Then he throws a dart into a wall map of the country and chooses one town in one state. Going there, he locates by random one name and address from the telephone book and calls up that number. The person contacted then has an opportunity to pull one emotional thread out of a highly complex life history, a story line that must end on an optimistic note, as required by the production values of the network. But the most obscene expression of the American as spectator, of the technological crafting of stories, was the House and Senate impeachment process of Bill Clinton. During the final days of the Senate trial, after the videotaped depositions of Monica Lewinsky, Vernon Jordan, and Sidney Blumenthal, the television-viewing world of spectators was invited to view the chamber of the United States Senate as a magisterial writing workshop. A series of Managers, acting as narrators, attempted to pull together a "story" about the interactions of the three deposed witnesses with Bill Clinton. Video clips of individualized question-and-answer sessions with the three witnesses added "dialogue." The spectators observed a "story" being written, but one with no real meaning or moral value, given the trivial matter at its basis.

The ancient Greek was a spectator of a different sort. He attended the theater on a weekly basis in order to contemplate the fundamental ethical issues of his reality being dramatized by Aeschylus, Aristophanes, Euripides, and Sophocles. He watched to see who and what he was and what life itself meant. The Greeks had an earnestness and great intensity, and a deeply tragic sense of life. They avoided the trite and the commonplace and anything that had nothing to teach.

It may well be that the young writers now entering workshops have already been trained, by the technological media, as spectators. But this does not make them Greek-like. While it remains a human truth that people live in terms of images, it is also true that where there are no good images there will always be bad ones. And the images that, day after day, condition all of us are mostly drawn from the extreme, unmetaphorical range of the visual spectrum, evoking no recognition of moral complexity or depth. We have come to accept the mundane image, and its lack of human vitality, as only what should be expected, and are sometimes even bothered by the passionate, the perfected, the aspiration toward the ideal. The general culture has forged a kind of unconscious consensus with respect to the proper precincts in which beauty, and therefore truth and goodness, may be located. Given this reality, it seems to me that there should arise a challenge to this status quo from within those communities of writers whose job it is to expand the spectrum of acceptable images steeped in moral and metaphysical meanings.

Opportunities for such expansions can come from the most unexpected of places. Three summers ago, for example, the major newspapers carried a story and a picture of a young black woman in Ann Arbor, Michigan, who threw herself across the body of an American Nazi and took the blows that a group of attackers had intended for him. This image came into general consciousness and then faded out of it very quickly, but it told a story as deeply felt as the trial in Jasper, Texas, that is just concluding as of this writing. The roots of both stories go deep, and only radical acts of human sympathy could provide them with meaning and value. Once again, any effort to understand both incidents would require the writer to consider the increasing role now being played by the electronic media in assigning values to human groupings. I am alluding here to the increasing commodification of the "moral voice" by the mass media. Very serious concerns—the moral legacy of Martin Luther King Jr., issues of sexual and personal identity—are reduced to one-dimensional images and marketed to targeted groups as products. Perhaps it is this commercially driven reinforcement of group-specific demographics that has encouraged the reappearance of phratric communities—blacks, gays, feminists, white males, senior citizens—many of which groups, like the citizens of Corinth, Athens, and Sparta, were uncomfortable with each other. In Jasper, Texas, last summer a human being, called a white supremacist, helped to drag a black man to his death. In Wyoming, also last summer, and also just as impersonally, a group of ruffians killed a young gay man. The phratric community represented by the anti-abortionists maintain a website listing the names of the doctors and their families, members of an opposing phratric community, who perform abortions. Each time an abortionist is killed, a line, a very impersonal one, is drawn through his or her name on the website. Such events are usually casually reported and are received with numbness except by those belonging to the group being victimized. Each collectivized communal voice is given sufficient time to vent, or rant, their rage. Such ritual moments become, after a while, almost normative in their flatness or thinness, even to writers whose craft encourages them to wrestle their imaginations into such moments in order to locate whatever meaning, tragic or otherwise, resides in them.

The riot at Ann Arbor, in other words, was a typical confrontation between members of two radical phratric communities—the American Nazi Party and the remnants of the New Left. Ever since the early 1980s the American Nazis, almost always on the cutting edge of new trends, concluded that they were not recruiting enough new members through simple mailings of party propaganda. The Nazis were the first to foresee the propaganda potential in the new technologies—computers, video cameras, the Internet, the hunger of the media for unusual images. During those years the Nazis began targeting those campuses said to be populated by liberals. These sites were targeted as backdrops against which racial demonstrations would be made. The ruling assumption behind this strategy was that the liberal elements would turn out en masse and subject the Nazis to violent attacks, which would be dutifully filmed by the media and used to recruit new members of the party. This strategy worked all during the

1980s and 1990s until the Nazis ran into *meaning* in Ann Arbor, in the person of a young black woman who might have been a *spectator* in a comparable engagement in the South or elsewhere. Perhaps it was the moral training that a comparable spectacle had induced in her that she had the courage to turn away from it. Her body, thrown across the back of a fallen Nazi, said a resounding "No" to the theatricals of both the liberals and the Nazis. Because she remained human for a moment, her gesture, for a while, reminded a great number of people that transcendent loyalties could still exist outside of the phratric sense of self. She made a genuinely *human* gesture, one worthy of literary engagement, because it restored something of beauty to the world.

Now, some years later, the citizens of Jasper, Texas, faced with the consequence of another calculated gesture, have affirmed the rightness of the Ann Arbor woman's gesture. Assigned the role of spectators, they chose to remain conscious of transcendent images, of justice or of compassion, toward the other extreme of the media-saturated spectrum, where adequate images reside.

III

In late May of 1998 I drove from Bristol, Rhode Island, into Cambridge, Massachusetts, with a group of Japanese friends. We had lunch in a restaurant just across from Harvard Yard and then walked around Harvard Square. Over in Harvard Yard, just at that time, President Neil L. Rudenstine was giving his Commencement Address, and there was a great crowd of people, students and their families, packed in. As my friends and I walked along the edge of the crowd, I listed to President Rudenstine's voice over the public address system. I kept hearing him repeat the word *values*. I had not attended my own graduation from Harvard in 1968, and so, thirty years later, I lingered on the edge of the crowd, listening to the speech and pretending that it represented the distillation of wisdom I had missed back in 1968. After I returned to Iowa City, I received in June a copy of *Harvard Magazine* containing the full text of the speech. It was called "The Nature of the Humanities," and in it President Rudenstine expressed his fear that the humanities are in danger of being eclipsed by the natural sciences and the social sciences. He made an eloquent case for the essential place the humanities have for the health of society as a whole. While conceding that the humanities are untidy, offering knowledge not susceptible to elegant proofs, and thrive on the pattern, texture, and flow of experience, they nonetheless provide the most vital signs of human experience as any other representation. Rudenstine added:

> The purpose is not so much closure along a single line of inquiry—as we might find in the sciences—but illuminations that are hard won because they can only be discovered in the very midst of life, with all its vicissitudes. If we are fortunate and alert, we may gradually learn how to see more clearly the nature and possible meaning of events; to be better attuned to the nuances, inflections, and character of other human beings; to weigh values with more precision; to judge on the basis on increasingly fine distinctions; and perhaps to become more effective, generous, and wise in our actions. . . .

He also made a case for the interrelatedness of great literature to the more practical work of a society—that reading Plato's *Republic* opens questions about political theory and practice and law and civic obligations. "When it comes to central questions of the meaning of human life," he told the audience, "neither the humanities, the sciences, nor the social sciences can be sovereign."

President Rudenstine's speech led me to reconsider my own role as a teacher in a workshop setting, where I have been making a living for well over twenty-five years. During those years of contact with young writers from a great diversity of ethnic, educational, and regional backgrounds, I have had to educate myself, over and over, in the cultures and values of people from points of origin different from my own. I have had to do a great amount of reading, of self-education, in order to better communicate with the students whom I profess to teach. Since I began my teaching career at the University of California at Santa Cruz, back in 1969, I had developed the habit of spontaneously lending books to students. At first such gestures might have grown out of my own desire to be professorial. ("I'm the teacher because I've read the book!") But gradually, over the years, I have come to realize that by maintaining a "floating library" of books lent out, I was sometimes able to touch a student just at a time when an insight expressed in a specific book might be of help in the clarification of values. More than this, the great range of academic backgrounds brought by young writers into the workshops made it easier for a physics major to discuss theories of causality with a major in religion. It became easier for a writer trained in the exact language of law to learn the emotional language of fiction and poetry from a peer. A medical doctor could learn mythology from a classmate who had been educated in the classics. A writer with a background in engineering could, just by conversing with a music major, learn how American technology and American music derive from the very same idiom. A student with a background in film could help his classmates master the essentials of narrative pacing. Best of all, I, as a teacher, could gain wider knowledge from such a diverse body of students.

This is the kind of cross-fertilization, or of abstraction and recombination, that writing workshops can offer, even at a time when the outside society is becoming increasingly specialized and technological in its aesthetic and spiritual precincts. Such enclaves represent the ideal places for the conferring of affirmative action on people who have possession of the artful artifacts, like Lucius Mummius, but who need to learn just how they relate to rituals grounded in passion and the quest for what is beautiful in life, especially in a life as relentlessly materialistic as American life currently is. Once again, it is only a matter of clarifying the often ignored spectrum of adequate images, and investing them with meaning and with value. An example comes to mind from an incident three or four years ago. One student had asked me to work with him in an independent study on religion. After I agreed, several of his peers asked if they could join us. Then other students asked to join the group. Marilynne Robinson, my colleague, agreed to help me teach what was becoming a class. A sign-up list was posted on a bulletin board, and it was soon filled with the names of young fiction writers and poets. Even some Mormon missionaries came to the classes. As for myself, as one of the teachers, I was obliged to study in order to increase my own knowledge of religion. The larger point is that, within all such gatherings of talented and curious people, such extensions of the spectrum of adequate images can take place. In such projections of communal imagination, deeper meanings can be explored, meanings that may give beauty and passion and depth to the fiction written out of this experience of exploration.

Finally, such communities of talented writers have an opportunity to impose their own values on the technological and marketing revolutions that have already taken place. Once a new technique has been introduced, it can either be ignored or else it can be embraced and made to serve one's own purposes. The new technology, as always, is neutral; it is, finally, the user who must determine its highest value. For example, the marketing of books by Amazon.com on the Internet, the trade in sharply discounted books by Barnes and Noble and by Daedalus, while putting great economic pressures on independent booksellers, also makes many important books cheaper to purchase. Once again, the encouragement of levels of taste, or the discernment of beauty, encourages an appreciation of books that are outside commercial concern but are simply available. Great classics can easily be purchased at discount. The purely commercial books can be ignored. Similarly, the introduction of the VCR has encouraged many classic films to be remastered, reedited, and made available, also at great discount. Anyone can now build his own library of great films, once again ignoring those without sufficient aesthetic or moral content. The same is true of the relation of the compact disc to the cultivation of taste in music. The basic fact is that no one is really obliged to compromise a passion for aesthetic perfection, a passion for the ideal, on the altars of commercial taste. One can simply look the other way, toward where the ideal should reside.

These are some of the benefits of the new technology for writers and artists. For better or for worse, it has provided twenty-first-century people with what Andre Malraux called, two generations ago, a "museum without walls." That is, most people now have at their disposal reproductions of much of the great art produced in human history—books, paintings, music—as well as an understanding of the rituals and meanings behind them. Marilynne Robinson would caution here that during the last decades of this century we have begun to celebrate merely the surface of those meanings without any understanding of their content, historical or otherwise. But perhaps this is only the nature of change, only the lapse in time between the Triumph Lucius Mummius received when he hauled his carts of loot into Rome from destroyed Corinth. It is possible that, in succeeding years, sensibilities superior to the Roman General's developed a deeper appreciation of the culture that produced the beautiful artifacts. Perhaps, finally, this is the role that the many, many writing workshops are destined to play. In my view, they will remain the places where the best of the literary resources of the humanities will remain available to those who want to develop refined levels of taste and meaning that will help define some ultimate meanings, no matter what else is being marketed outside such enclaves. It will be simply a matter of imagining the other way.

The Dead Man

Not dead, yet: We found him where he had tried to die in his car—a huge old Mercedes pulled to the side of Reservoir Road, a washed-out dirt track encircling, what else, a reservoir. It was a damp morning in early spring of 1973, a time of year we liked to call "mud season"; I noticed the man in the driver's seat first as we passed, taking the turn slowly, because of the mud. His white head lay with an ominous stillness on the wheel. I told my father to stop.

We were on our way to buy a hammer, not because a hammer is symbolic, but because that was what we needed. Things were still good in my family, the troubles with money and all the rest had yet to arrive, and my father and I had been passing the morning trying to build a birdhouse, when the head of the hammer he was using flew clean off, arcing over his shoulder to clang harmlessly across the cement floor of the cold garage. This was in the town where I was raised, the town of my parents' unhappy exile, in upstate New York; I was eleven years old. We had moved there from Boston when I was five, after the end of the family business, an event that meant nothing to me except that I left one life behind and started another.

I looked behind us to the Mercedes. It was parked at a careless angle, half in the ditch, where water ran freely. The front end and quarter panels were dented haphazardly and streaked with blemishes of rust.

"You think he's okay?" I asked.

My father lifted his eyes to the rearview mirror. Still, no motion in the car behind us.

"It's a funny place to take a nap."

"Maybe he didn't see us," I offered.

My father undid his seat belt. His face was grim. "Wait here."

Outside, my father zipped up his orange slicker—he had once been a sailor of some accomplishment, the captain of a college team that sent several men to the Olympics, and all his coats and jackets were meant to be worn in storms at sea—and strode purposefully through a drizzly rain back to the Mercedes. I tried my best to obey, but couldn't. Hadn't I been the one to see the Mercedes first? I counted to ten and joined him at the car, where my father was rapping on the closed driver-side window.

"You there," he was saying in a loud voice. "Hello? Hello?"

In my memory the first thing I noticed when my father opened the door was the smell—a dank pungency of earth and closed air and sour breath, strange and familiar at once. It was so strong I closed my eyes against it, and then opened them again to look. I saw that the man at the wheel was an older man, many years older than my father, who was 36—the age I am now. Despite his awkward posture, slumped at the wheel, I could tell that he was slender and very tall; I thought that he must have liked the Mercedes for the room it gave his long legs. His hair, greasy and white, lay in a solid shape over his forehead. More tufts of white hair sprouted in his ears. He was wearing a suit coat, but only a tee shirt beneath it, and khaki slacks stained in a dark circle where he had pissed himself. I had been around drinkers and drunks all my life, not knowing they were different from anybody else, nor that their loud voices, broad gestures, sharp aromas, and expansive landscapes of feeling were anything out of the ordinary. But this was obviously something else entirely.

"What's the matter with him?"

My father glanced at me but didn't answer. With tender care—he had been a medical student, though never a doctor—he eased the man's face back from the wheel. A pendulum of saliva swayed from his lips. His eyes were bloody eggs, open but uncomprehending.

"Poor bastard," my father said. "He's out like a light."

The man's lips began to work, though his eyes had closed again. My father leaned in to listen. It was then that I saw the nearly empty bottle of Scotch, lolling on the floor beneath the passenger seat. I recognized the brand; it was the one my parents drank.

"What's he saying?"

My father backed out of the car. "Never mind that."

The man's voice was suddenly clear. "Bitch," he said. A bubble of spittle formed on his damp lips. "Thaaaa ... bitch."

I had no idea what to make of this, and having said his piece, the man in the Mercedes fell silent again. My father took his wrist and counted off his pulse. He was good in a crisis—still good, I should say—and I liked watching him, his cool efficiency and purposefulness, and the feeling it gave me as I stood by the car that I would be able to rely on him if I ever really needed to. We were not a family to whom anything truly awful had yet happened, and when it did finally happen it caught us all completely by surprise. But back then I viewed my father, as many boys do, as the net that lay beneath me, beneath us all.

"This isn't good," he announced. The rain had briefly stopped, and he took this moment to look across the reservoir to the dark hills beyond. All the trees were dripping, their branches blackened with moisture. "He needs an ambulance. I think he might have taken some pills, too."

"The Priors live up the road." Ben Prior was a friend from school. His father was a banker; their house was huge, and had a pool with a slide.

"How far?"

I pointed in the direction we'd come. "Just over the hill. We come down here sometimes."

We agreed that I would go and make the call. Then my father did something that surprised me. He reached inside the car, over the man's lap—I thought for a moment that he was going to perform CPR—and seized the whiskey bottle from the floor. Without examining it, or trying to conceal the gesture from me at all, he slid the bottle into one of the deep pockets of his slicker.

"Get a move on," my father said.

I looked at the man in the car again. "Do we know him?" I asked.

"No," my father answered. "We don't. Now go."

I took off at a run. I understood, in some feeling way, what my father was doing with the whiskey—that by taking the bottle he meant to do the man a kindness, though of what sort I didn't know. That the man in the car was a stranger compounded the mysterious urgency of this gesture, and my sense that my father and I, on this rainy morning, had been thrust together on a mortal mission to save not just a life but a reputation, a public history, a story—the most serious thing of all. By the time I got to the Priors I was winded and perspiring and could barely get the words out as I tried to explain to the housekeeper, the only person home, who I was and what I wanted. She left me standing at the door while she telephoned emergency services, and by the time I returned to the car, a sheriff's deputy had arrived, and then directly the EMTs, who wasted no time strapping the man to a gurney and carting him off under a bleeping siren. Maybe an hour had passed since we'd found him. I didn't ask about the whiskey, knowing it was a secret, but also because I understood what had become of it: it was in the woods somewhere.

By the side of the road, the deputy questioned my father, jotting notes onto a pad. The questions he asked were harmless and ordinary—when had we found him, had he said anything, how could my father be reached at a later time if necessary—and then the deputy told us we were free to go.

"You should be proud of yourself," he said to me, returning his notepad to his jacket pocket. He was an immense and solid man, like a weight lifter, and in his quasi-military uniform and broad-brimmed hat dripping with rain he exuded a calm and magisterial presence. "You probably saved that man's life, you know. A lot of people wouldn't have stopped."

He turned to my father, who seemed tiny beside him. "That's a good boy you have there. Sharp eyes."

My father nodded, but seemed not to hear him. He was squinting down the road, his eyes tracing the invisible course of the departed ambulance. For a moment, we both watched him.

He turned then, lifting one hand in a gesture that seemed to go nowhere. "The dead man . . . ," he began.

His face paled with alarm; his eyes were open very wide, and he looked close to tears. "God, how awful," he said to himself. "The dead man."

He tried to compose himself but failed at once. He stumbled forward, overcome, his body slackening like a deflating balloon; the deputy held out his arms to catch him by the shoulders as he fell. The moment felt frozen, an image etched in time: The deputy bracing my father upright with his arms, my father in his luminous orange slicker, his chin on his chest, all power drained from him.

My father stiffened. "I'm all right," he said then, stepping away.

The deputy took him by the elbow. "Maybe we better get you off your feet a second."

My father let the deputy steer him to the bumper of his cruiser, where he obediently sat. His face blazed with embarrassment.

"It's really nothing," my father insisted. "I don't know why I said that. I meant the man in the car. I just wanted to know what hospital they'd take him to."

The deputy eyed him cautiously. "You're sure you don't know him?"

My father shook his head and looked away. "I have no idea who that was."

This was twenty-five years ago, and of course it's really a story about my father—maybe the one story. And so it is also a story about writing.

I think of the two simultaneously, because my father was a writer, or should have been. Before he was unlucky in business, he was unlucky in law, and before that, medicine; his lifelong search for something to do, something suitable, took him from one misery to another and finally no place at all. But in college he had been a writer, and a fine one. More than fine: He was an absolute natural. This was the last great heyday of American comic writing, when wit and erudition still counted for something, and my father's work was nothing short of Thurber-esque. He had been a regular contributor to the campus humor magazine, the *Harvard Lampoon,* and the issues in which his work appeared were stacked with reverential wistfulness on the shelves of his den, beside the oxidizing sailing trophies that also dated from the same period. By the time I got to them, their pages were brittle and yellow, crisped at the edges like papers plucked from a fire. I poured over them for hours: stories with titles like "Mr. Rabbit at the Ritz"; long, doggerel poems poking brutal fun at every Ivy pretension; wonderfully inventive fables, including two small masterpieces I remember as if I'd read them yesterday, one about a moth living in the muffler of a Park Avenue debutante, the other about a lamprey who affixes himself to the side of an oil tanker and tries to drink it dry. They were full of cleverness, full of joy, and remembering them now, I know that my father could have "made it." His stories and poems possessed a confident charm that can't be learned, an affinity for language as natural as the lung's taste for breath, and I'm certain that he loved writing them. His college yearbook lay on the same shelf as the magazines, and perusing its pages I came across a candid photo of him, shot in the Lampoon

Castle on Mt. Auburn Street. My father, twenty-one years old, campus cutup and Algonquin wit-in-waiting, black-haired and youthfully trim, a Winston clamped in his teeth; he is standing beside two fellow editors, the three of them laughing their handsome heads off at the latest issue of the magazine. A clock on the wall behind them says that it's two o'clock—no doubt, two A.M.— and there is my father, utterly alive. It is probably the truest photo of him that was ever taken.

Who knows why he stopped? Writing is hard, almost no one thanks you for it, you can make more money doing almost anything else if you do it at all well. It's easy enough to find reasons not to write, and it's possible that my father never knew just how good he was—that no one told him he could give his life to something he actually loved to do. Without meaning to, he had found the work he was meant for; then, like a character in one of his own fables, he walked away and spent the rest of his life roaming the earth in search of it. He descended into sour silence, punctuated by outbursts of focusless anger, and by the time I was old enough to ask him what I might do for a living, even I knew I was asking only as a courtesy. In college, when I announced my own intentions to be a writer, he sent me a crate of paper, with these words written on the side: "Contents: Unwritten novel. Handle with high hope." From somebody else, it might have been encouraging, and it nearly was. Not much later, his ship taking on water faster than even he could bail, his parting words to me were these: "You go to hell forever, you little bastard."

I have lived long enough to know that sometimes good people meet bad or sloppy ends, that sometimes nothing works out despite what's promising about us. I know it now, but I began to learn it on Reservoir Road, beside the parked Mercedes. The deputy was right, and my father, too; we had saved the driver's life. His veins were full of whiskey and barbiturates, a cocktail of lethal bitterness, and en route to the emergency room, the paramedics shocked his heart back to life not once but twice. How this news made its way to me I can't say. Probably my parents told me, or else I overheard them speaking of it. I never learned anything else about him, not even his name.

Did we do him a favor, there on the side of the road? What became of him, in the life we restored him to without asking? I have a single memory of seeing him later, and knowing it was he. I cannot explain this memory—it is so thoroughly improbable it could easily be a dream—and yet its details possess the insistent clarity of reality. A party at Christmas: I am standing on an interior balcony, like a choir loft, wearing a blue suit and flirting with the dark-haired girl beside me, a friend of my sister's home from boarding school for the holidays. I have just been awarded a scholarship of my own to Phillips Andover—the beginnings of my escape—and it is this synchronicity that leads me to believe, despite what is obviously true, that I might be able to pull off something interesting with her. My father is already absent, moving into his widening orbit, and I have, for the time being, given my mother the slip. The girl and I are drinking plastic cups of sour wine that we have harvested from the dozens of half-finished glasses left carelessly about by the grown-ups milling around the open floor below us. I am about to accept a cigarette from her—both astonished by my own bravery and worried that she will know I have never smoked before—when my eyes, perusing the crowd of party-goers like a shelf of books I might someday read, alight on a man I know at once is the man in the Mercedes.

He is a striking figure, dressed in a navy blazer and white pants with creases as sharp as a razor, and tall as I imagined he would be. His white hair is oiled—it glimmers faintly under the overhead lights—and combed away from his temples, revealing an architecture of patrician facial bones as precise as the creases of his pants, though the effect is blurred by the watery puffiness and veiny patina of the lifelong steady drinker. He is speaking to a woman I don't recognize, holding a glass of wine with one hand and cupping his ear with the other, to cull her words from the din of the party that moves around them like waves around a pier. He is, in sum, the very image of the country aristocrat, a holder of lands and trusts, somebody who in the small world of that town would have been considered important, a man of consequence. I am about to say something—maybe, even, to call out to him—when suddenly he laughs; or rather, he tosses his head back, opens his mouth toward the ceiling, and issues a single joyful and unrepentant bark. And my heart floods with a dark and happy power. I am the holder of his secret, the story of his direst hour, and yet he has no awareness of me at all. It is an overwhelming feeling, completely new; it is the feeling I have always longed for, of stepping into life.

I never saw him again, and it is ten years since I saw my father last; like the man in the Mercedes, he has been gone from my life so long that he has moved into the rooms of memory. I have no idea where he is now, or what he would say to me, but what I would say is this: that writing is the gift I meant to give him, the only one I could think of, and I chose it that day on the side of the road when I saw him in the deputy's arms and knew that he would die unfinished. He saw himself in that Mercedes, and I saw him—the whole history of my father, bottled in a moment—and I vowed to give him back his life somehow, to consecrate it by writing. I mean nothing less: Writing is a gift we carry back to our ancestors, like fire. It is the work we give the dead. We never spoke of the man in the car, my father and I. I have tried to tell the story, first to myself, then to anyone who would listen. I tell it now to him.

Twenty-five years, Dad. Here it is.

ABRAHAM VERGHESE

Cowpaths

For some time now I have flitted back and forth between medicine and writing as if I were a debutante stringing along two suitors. As a very young child, I announced that I wanted to be a journalist. My parents were both physicists, and my brothers were whizzes at math—my older brother is now a professor at MIT, and the other brother is a computer engineer with Hewlett-Packard—but I clearly had no head for sums. I sensed, however, that for me there was safety in words; words were my allies. Numbers, equations, and theorems were (and remain) completely opaque and intimidating. I'm sure my parents were disappointed by my stated career choice; middle-class Indian families consider only two professions to be worthy of their offspring: medicine and engineering.

In my early teens I abandoned the idea of journalism, and it was all because of Somerset Maugham's *Of Human Bondage*. Something about Maugham's protagonist, Philip, who failed at art (not the writing kind, but the paint-on-canvas kind) and turned to medicine, made medicine seem to me a passionate pursuit, the equal of art, but safer. Even the most diligent artist might discover that he or she had no talent. By contrast, with hard work one could generally succeed in medicine. And there was little math involved with the study of medicine; it had more to do with words, and with, as Maugham wrote, the study of "humanity, there in the rough."

I remember that my medical school experience began with the dissection of the upper limb. I propped my *Gray's Anatomy* against the shoulder of the shriveled woman whose corpse I shared with four others, and I began to read about the brachial plexus, the complex bundle of nerves that emerged from the spinal cord to innervate the upper limb. Not only could I make perfect sense of the description, but I could see the brachial plexus in my mind's eye, as if the words were building blocks that stacked themselves up just so. Over the next few weeks, as we took scalpel to skin, one day, there before our eyes was the brachial plexus, just as I had imagined it, and just as the book had described it. What a wonderful affirmation of the power and the tangible nature of words! Who has ever stripped flesh and seen a theorem? Who has found a differential equation lurking beneath a blood vessel?

Something strange happened when I qualified as a physician and began postgraduate training, first in internal medicine, and then later in the subspecialty of infectious diseases. I noticed that my patients' stories of their illness—what exactly they were doing when the symptoms began, what they thought and felt and feared, what their neighbors said it might be, and how the startling sight of blood in the urine (for example) broke through their denial, their wish to label this "indigestion"—bore no resemblance to the language I recorded in the chart. My medical training had reduced their colorful tale to "this forty-year-old Hispanic female with a past history of cholecystitis and hypothyroidism presents with a three-week history of flank pain radiating to the groin, one week of dysuria, and one day of hematuria." This stripping of the sickness narrative of its personal context, of whatever made it truly the patient's, reflects what Walker Percy called "cowpaths"—the narrow ruts of language and thought that characterize professional medical training. Such language—the voice of medicine—is efficient and necessary for diagnosis, but its downside is that it makes it easy for physicians to stop fully imagining the patient's suffering. It makes it difficult to see a patient as unique, since every story undergoes this reductive process. I think that was when my urge to write reawakened. I had learned the voice of medicine, but I wanted to capture the voice of the patient.

When, in the mid-1980s, my practice began to revolve around the care of persons dying with AIDS, I found that writing short fictional pieces in the evenings represented one means by which to change those things that in the daytime I could not change. There is a definition of poetry (and, by extension, fiction) that I like; it states that poetry is "… a means of achieving one kind of success at the limits of the ability of the will to express itself by other means." The limits of my will as a physician were altogether too evident: I could not turn back time, I could not prevent the CD4 cell counts from declining, I could not get into my patients' heads, and ultimately, I could not prevent the inexorable downhill trajectory of their disease. At night, however, by the vehicle of fiction, I could do all these things: I could get into their heads, I could turn back time, I could keep people alive.

I took to heart the message my patients seemed to be conveying to me on their deathbeds: they seemed to be saying very clearly, don't postpone your dreams. In 1990, I applied to the Iowa Writers' Workshop, sent in my two stories, and when I was accepted, I took that as a clear signal to go. I cashed in my retirement, left my tenured position at a medical school, and went off to Iowa.

I was in for a culture shock in Iowa. I remember feeling completely inadequate during that first workshop meeting (we met just once a week). After fifteen years spent single-mindedly studying medicine, I could barely follow what was being said. The terms being bandied about by my new classmates—most of whom were younger and had come straight out of prestigious English programs—were completely foreign to me: *deconstruc-*

tion, Barth, Cheeveresque. That first semester I checked out a dozen library books each week, reading furiously, trying to learn this new rhetoric. Only at the end of the semester did I realize that there was no correlation (perhaps even an inverse correlation) between being an erudite lit-crit maven, a brilliant deconstructor of someone else's work, and the quality of one's own fiction.

Once a week, during my stay in Iowa, I worked at the University of Iowa's AIDS clinic. That was a respite, a setting where the language and the rituals were much more familiar. It served also to remind me that if I had something going for me as a writer, it was that as a physician, I had been privy to many extraordinary situations—I had seen humanity in the rough, and there was much to write about. Though there were and always will be some amazingly gifted and precocious young writers in the Workshop, it seemed to me that some modicum of life experience outside of a college campus was an advantage to a writer, perhaps even a prerequisite for good writing.

The Workshop never claimed to teach writing; there was no system one could follow, no dogma (unlike in medicine) to memorize and hang your hat on. But what the Workshop did was give me permission to write, permission to take myself seriously as a writer. It gave me the opportunity to have my peers as well as some of the extraordinary faculty respond to my writing and point out to me all my failings. It also gave me time, a huge chunk of time to read and write. I was in my late thirties then and had two young children—I knew how precious time to write was, and how I could not afford to waste it. I didn't think I would ever have the luxury of that kind of time again, four semesters worth. Oh, I attended many of the parties, drank more than my share, went to all the readings, but for the most part I tried to perfect the attribute that I thought best characterized a writer: the discipline of applying my ass to the chair.

I am sometimes asked whether I see myself primarily as a doctor or a writer. The truth is, I have come increasingly to see them as one seamless whole. As an internist, a diagnostician, I am struck at how often, when I am consulted on a difficult patient, it is not some special skill, some esoteric knowledge that I bring to the bedside that solves the case. Rather, what I do is take the patient's history a little better perhaps than the intern. After all, what is a hi-story but a story? I milk the history; I extract meaning from it, try to see if its pattern matches my repository of stories; I make inferences from the story. Then when I pull the sheet back to see what story the body tells, once again I unearth more clues than the intern does, perhaps because I have come to expect them, I have faith that they are there. I have seen the patterns, the familiar beginnings and endings, the plot twists, even the clichés of disease. I am struck by the fact that I heard the same aphorism in medical school and at the Writers' Workshop: "God is in the details." To me those qualities—being painstaking, being a bit obsessive, getting the significant details right—are fundamental to sound doctoring and good writing.

When I write fiction, I find myself driven by the urge to avoid the usual cowpaths and the well-worn ruts. No stories set on college campuses, please! I am drawn to characters and voices that are uncommon, even bizarre. I am conscious of anatomy, and how anatomy is physiology, something Dickens understood so well: The corpulent character has a different world view than the lean ascetic one. I am intrigued by the dichotomy between what the cognitive mind of a character claims to want and what he or she is driven to do—it is precisely the kind of lunatic alchemy that one sees in the real world. Yes, the cognitive mind knows about safe sex and condoms, but when passion is stoked, it is not the cognitive mind that is driving the bus; some other part takes over. Death is omnipresent in my fiction, but I don't think of this as an aberration. I would even argue that it is perhaps the most realistic aspect of my fiction; after all, what other part of a life story is more certain than its ending? And should a disease appear in my stories (and it often does) it must have meaning for the character, because that too is human nature: we tend to ascribe meaning and metaphor to our illness; we tend to refute science and mere chance, and we assume that one thing is connected to another. As a writer, I want my reader to be the diagnostician. My job is to provide the telling clues and trust the reader to come to a diagnosis, and to arrive at it with a certain satisfaction.

To serve both my mistresses well is difficult and at times downright frustrating. Yet I am not sure that if I had a lakeside cabin and a year to write (but not see patients) that I would have very much to say. Even worse would be to find myself in a Doc-in-the-box, nine-to-five job without the opportunity to record words other than the standard illness narrative in the prescribed squares on the HMO encounter sheet, without the opportunity to teach and demonstrate to students, without the chance to reflect on what I see, without the leisure of finding out what that experience means.

That is why I write: because I still find comfort in words, because I find safety in the structures one can build from words, and because it is only by writing that I discover exactly what it is I am thinking.

CHRIS OFFUTT

The Eleventh Draft

I didn't set out to be a writer. In chronological order, I wanted to be a baseball player, an explorer, a race car driver, a detective, a movie actor, an artist, and a forest ranger. I was a voracious reader as a child, consuming several books a week. At age ten, I asked the town librarian for a book about baseball and she gave me *Catcher in the Rye*. What I recall most is the shock that writing could be that way—personal, told in an intimate way, about family issues of supreme importance. I never read another book for juveniles.

In grade school, I kept diaries that detailed problems I had with Billy, a neighbor who lived across the creek and was a consummate bully. In Spelling class I wrote stories about battles between two knights—Sir Christophoro and Sir Billyano. Billy beat me in real life, but in the world of fiction, Sir Christophoro always won.

After leaving my native Kentucky, I spent nearly a decade working part-time jobs around the country. My writing was confined to a journal, in which I wrote an average of 30 pages a day. I usually wrote in public—on benches, in buses and trains, in restaurants and bars. It was important that people saw me writing. The perception of strangers granted a feeling of self-worth, an identity as a struggling young writer.

I began collecting photographs of my favorite writers, which I studied carefully. My greatest admiration was reserved for those writers whose faces reflected the most suffering. In my early twenties I felt that I didn't deserve to be a writer due to a lack of genuine experience, and I became grateful for the acne pocks on my jaws and the scar between my eyes. These marks of life lent the illusion of being a writer. I bought a typewriter for two hundred dollars, the most money I'd spent on an item. One day, I removed the mirror from the bathroom and fastened it to the wall above my typewriter. Around the mirror I taped the photographs of my favorite writers. When I sat at the typewriter, my face joined theirs.

If I wasn't writing, I wasn't visible.

Writing is the most difficult task I've ever undertaken, which is perhaps why I do it. For much of my life, I cared about little except the act of writing. Writing taught me to trust myself, which enabled me to trust others. This resulted in marriage, and within a year my wife convinced me to apply to an MFA program. I did so reluctantly, and with no alternative. We'd moved back to Kentucky, where we were living without benefit of plumbing, heat, or jobs. The summer I turned thirty, we borrowed a thousand dollars and headed for Iowa. This decision literally changed my life.

We rented a condemned building near the jail. Daylight showed between the wall and the floor, and the landlord's solution was stapling sheets of plastic to the exterior wall. Our house looked like a giant bread sack. The bedroom ceiling eventually fell in, but Rita and I were happy. The new place had water and a furnace. We'd moved up.

Several years before, while living in Salem, Massachusetts, I enrolled in a Dostoyevsky class through Harvard's continuing education. The class was small. A student assured me that the instructor was a genius. We sat for two hours discussing the first chapter of *Crime and Punishment,* a hundred-page section, which I'd read twice in preparation. I was excited as only a naive country boy can be who had fought his way out of the Appalachian Mountains and into a Harvard extension program. At the end of class I left without a word to anyone. I was ashamed and embarrassed. Though I had listened carefully, I had no idea what anyone was talking about.

At Iowa, I was fearful of undergoing the same experience. The majority of my classmates held degrees in English, and possessed a unique vocabulary for the analysis and discussion of writing. Many of them were graduates of private schools. Having never taken a writing class, I was intimidated, envious, and terrified. My brain and my interests had always made me feel like an outsider, and slowly I realized that the other students felt the same way. For the first time in my life I was around people like me—devoted to the twin acts of reading and writing. Class, race, and education didn't matter. I'd spent a lifetime learning to conceal my intellect, reign in my vocabulary, and guard my personality. In Iowa I was allowed to be smart. For many years I had taken writing very seriously, but now I took myself seriously as a writer.

A first draft was like a wonderful drug that made me feel good. Revision was the horrible crash. For years I avoided the crash by refusing to revise. In order to generate a first draft, I staked everything on the act of writing. My identity and emotional well-being went into each page, paragraph, sentence, and word. Making a single change was like a surgeon performing a complex procedure on his own heart. I found it impossible.

At Iowa, I overcame this problem by simply starting a new story. Once I was emotionally involved with a fresh piece of writing, I could return to the first one with the necessary distance. It became important to have several stories underway, because work on one was always going badly. I then turned to another until becoming overwhelmed, at which time I worked on a third, and so on. The only rule I had was to complete a first draft before revising. When I switched my focus to another story, I gave the entire manuscript a full revision. To my utter surprise, I began to accumulate story manuscripts. They were never completed, merely abandoned, a practice I still maintain.

Being among a community of writers granted me permission to write what scared me most—stories about people in Appalachia. These were essentially stories of myself, seen through the magnifying veil of my own experience in the world beyond the hills. After years of wanting to be someone else—an actor, a painter, a ranger—I suddenly realized that people are what they do, not what they want to be. And what I did was confront existence through language. I was no longer someone who wanted desperately to be. I had become someone who simply was—a writer.

The notion of submitting anything to a magazine filled me with terror. A stranger would read my precious words, judge them deficient, and reject them, which meant I was worthless. A poet friend was so astonished by my inaction that he shamed me into sending my stories out. My goal, however, was not publication, which was still too scary a thought. My goal was a hundred rejections in a year.

I mailed my stories in multiple submissions and waited eagerly for their return, which they promptly did. Each rejection brought me that much closer to my goal—a cause for celebration, rather than depression. Eventually disaster struck. The *Coe Review* published my first story in spring 1990. The magazine was in the small industrial town of Cedar Rapids, Iowa, with a circulation that barely surpassed the city limits. The payment was one copy of the magazine, and the editor spelled my name wrong. Nevertheless, I felt valid in every way—I was no longer a hillbilly with a pencil full of dreams. I was a real live writer.

The second year of school, I doubled my efforts—more discipline, more work, digging more deeply into my own life. We moved into a tiny house with a basement that was only accessible through a tornado hatch outside. I installed a plywood floor and a wall. Each morning I went outside, lifted the heavy door that was flat to the ground, and descended into my imagination. The light was dim, the walls were close, and the ceiling low. At day's end I emerged from the earth, squinting like a mole.

My process of writing had developed until I preferred the act of revision to first draft. I printed a story and made all my changes on paper. I then inserted those changes into the computer and printed it. My files were meticulous. Each draft was numbered and dated, and I kept them in chronological order. Often I went back to previous drafts, seeking a remembered line that I'd cut along with a paragraph. Occasionally I resurrected entire scenes that I'd trimmed.

The move to revision became so complete that I no longer cared about the story as product. What mattered was the evolution of the act of creation. I spent many joyful hours simply shifting material from one narrative to another, gauging the success of the integration, attempting greater risks on the page. Plot was a loose form I could rely on in the same way that poets might utilize a sonnet or villanelle.

The more I worked, the more I understood that a writer never really stops writing. Leaving my basement didn't end the process. I continued to write in my head. My relationship with the world was one of narrative, and I engaged life eagerly while simultaneously keeping a segment of my mind detached to notice sensory detail. My pockets filled with scraps of paper that held description of light and land, snippets of conversation, and observation of character. In my basement I organized the notes, typed them under various headings, and kept them close at hand.

My first drafts are very long. The second one is a rapid chop job of all the junk I threw in during the delirium of a first draft. The third revision is workable. I pare the story down and then fatten it up. Subsequent drafts are the same—fat one, thin one, fat one, thin one. The pattern is similar to the action of a bellows—expanding and contracting, forcing oxygen to the fire of narrative. The stories get shorter in length, but thicker in detail. I add and cut, trying to let the story dictate what it wants. My mind jumps from a ruthless objectivity to an intensely personal interaction with the story and then back to the emotional distance necessary to revision.

An average short story is a result of ten or eleven drafts over a two-year period. The longest is thirty-five versions written during eight years. It's an intensely autobiographical story, both in event and emotional content, with only the ending being written from scratch. The story was originally about my father and me. During the writing, I became a father, and the story shifted gears as my identity changed. The problem was simple—trying to control the actions of the characters. After I let them do what they wanted to do, the story quickly completed itself. I felt as if I had been on a train stalled in a rail yard that suddenly shot down the tracks with no warning. Instead of writing the story, I was a passenger.

As long as I am sitting at my desk with my imagination plugged into the world of my characters, I consider myself engaged in the act of writing. On a rare day, I'll write several pages, while other days only a page. There are times that require four hours to squeeze out a mere paragraph. The toughest writing sessions are those when not a word spills forth.

I regard all of these times as equal to one another and valid to the act of writing. Two words are the same as two pages. I am writing simply by virtue of allowing my mind to enter the world of my characters. If I go three days without writing a word, I know that the eventual sentences will be that much stronger for the time spent in the company of my characters.

The only way I can create anything worthwhile is to concern myself solely with the moment, to maintain as much freedom as possible during the interaction between my mind and narrative. This has led me to write what I need to write, instead of what I want to write. My work, both fiction and nonfiction, is about my current emotional state, my past behavior, and my recent thoughts. The years of revision enable me to understand myself.

The irony is that by the time I learn from my work, it's too late to do anything, because those difficulties are over and I'm in the midst of a whole new batch of problems.

Five years after moving to Iowa I was a father of two boys, and an author of two books. My sense of self had changed so drastically that I was at a loss of who I was anymore. My response was to write a novel about a man who leaves Kentucky, moves to Montana, and changes his identity right down to his name and Social Security number. To write it, I had a thousand-dollar yard sale and moved to Montana.

Today, ten years after Iowa, I have returned to Kentucky, where I am polishing galleys for *Out of the Woods*. It is a book of stories written over the past decade. Each story concerns someone from eastern Kentucky who has left and misses it. Some return and some don't. At this point I utterly despise the manuscript. It is the final stage before publication, and I'm reduced to changing commas to conjunctions and back to commas. I am perpetually dismayed by what the book says about me, although I cannot pinpoint any particular insight. Perhaps I can in the future. Until then, I am planning the next book.

In order to let this book go, I need to hate it, because I'll miss it so badly. Publication means snatching its life away. A part of me goes with it. Nothing will fill the absence but another project, another imaginary world. Nothing will save me but the act of writing.

CHARLES D'AMBROSIO

Seattle, 1974
Writing and Place

The initial salvos in my hankering to expatriate took the predictable route of firing snobby potshots at the local icons of culture, at Ivar with his hokey ukulele and Stan Boreson and Dick Balsch with his ten-pound sledge bashing cars and laughing like a maniac all through the late night, and so forth. (Actually I thought DB was cool, and so did a good many of my friends. He had the crude and sinister good looks of a porn star and once merited an admiring squib in *Time*. In his cheap improvised commercials—interrupting Roller Derby and the antics of Joannie Weston the Blonde Amazon—he'd beat brand-new cars with a hammer, so to me he always seemed superior to circumstance; our old cars just got beat to hell by life, whereas Dick Balsch went out on the attack. It was a period when a lot of us hero-worshipped people who destroyed things, and even now I wonder where DB's gone and half-hope he'll come back and smash more stuff.) Anyone born in geographical exile, anyone from the provinces, anyone for whom the movements of culture feel rumored, anyone like this grows up anxiously aware that all the innovative and vital events in the world happen Back East, like way back, like probably France, but before expatriation can be accomplished in fact it is rehearsed and performed in the head.

You make yourself clever and scoffing, ironic, deracinated, cold and quick to despise. You import your enthusiasms from the past, other languages, traditions. You make the voyage first in the aisles of bookstores and libraries, in your feckless dreams. The books you love best feature people who ditched their homes in the hinterlands for scenes of richer glory. Pretty soon the word *Paris* takes on a numinous quality and you know you won't be silent forever. Someday you'll leave.

Meanwhile, the only city I really knew was a dump worse than anything Julius Pierpont Patches (local TV clown) ever dreamed of, sunk in depression and completely off the cultural map, no matter what outlandish claims local boosters made for the region. And they made many. In a highly cherished book of mine *(You Can't Eat Mount Rainier*, by William Speidel, Jr., Bob Cram, illustrator, copyright 1955) I read, "What with the city's leading professional men, artists, writers, world travelers, and visiting VIPs always dropping into the place, [Ivar's] has become the spot where clams and culture meet." Huh? Artists? Writers? To explain, Ivar's is a local seafood restaurant, and Ivar himself was a failed folk singer in the tradition of the Weavers. Back then there was an abundance of clams and a paucity of culture, but even more than this disparity, I'd somehow arranged it in my head that clams, salmon, steelhead, and geoducks were actually antithetical to and the sworn enemies of culture. No one wrote about them, is what I probably meant. Perhaps clams and culture met, once, in 1955, but then of course 1955 stubbornly persisted in Seattle until, like, 1980, and inbetweentime you felt stuck mostly with mollusks. The culture side of the equation was most prominently represented by a handful of aging rearguard cornballs. Like Ivar himself.

If you were a certain type, and I was, you first had to dismantle the local scene's paltry offerings and then build up in its place a personal pantheon remote from the very notion that clams and culture really ever do meet, anywhere, at a time when, all arrogant and hostile and a budding prig, you believed culture was the proprietary right of a few Parisians. That an old warbly voiced yokel like Ivar might pass for culture, or that "Here Come the Brides" might signify to the world your sense of place, seemed a horror, an embarrassment. I went incognito, I developed alibis. For starters I took to wearing a black Basque beret and became otherwise ludicrously Francophile in my tastes. Mostly, however, I couldn't find solid purchase for my snobbism. Not that I didn't try. I'd have liked to be some old hincty Henry James but couldn't really sustain it. Still you badly wanted things delocalized, just a little. Even if you had to do it first just in your head, with issueless irony. You looked about. With a skeptical eye you sized up the offerings. You wondered, for instance, why it was that suddenly in Seattle there was aesthetic love of statues. You wondered, what is it with all these replicas of people around the region? A brass Ivar and his brass seagulls, some apparently homeless people (brass) in the courtyard of the James Sedgewick Bldg. (as if a real, non-brass loiterer could actually rest awhile on those benches unmolested), and then, last, least, a hideous band of five or six citizens (cement) waiting for the bus in Fremont. Like a bunch of gargoyles walked off their ancient job guttering rain, they've been waiting for the bus twenty or thirty years now. If you've lived here long enough (like a week) you know the rain of today is the rain of tomorrow and the rain of a million years ago, and if you stand in that eternal rain long enough and often enough you start to feel replicating the experience rubs it in your face. I've stood in the rain and waited for buses or whatever and it wasn't a joke, not that I understood, at least. You're standing there, you're buzzed, you're bored, you're waiting, you don't have a schedule, the rain's pounding around your head like nuthouse jibberjabber, and from this incessant and everlasting misery someone else works up an instance of passing cleverness and then casts it in concrete for all time?

Those stone citizens, silent and forever waiting, are like my nightmare.

I badly wanted to escape my unwritten city for a time and place already developed by words, for Paris or London or Berlin and a particular epoch as it existed in books. I wanted Culture, the upper-case sort. Books fit my minimum-wage budget and afforded the cheapest access. Fifty cents bought admission to the best. I purchased most of my early novels and poems from a woman who, I recall, only had one leg. Later there was Elliot Bay Books, which offered both a bookstore and a brick-walled garret in the basement. You could loiter without having to skulk. You could bring your empty cup to the register and ask for refills. And you could read. Those books, more than any plane ticket, offered a way out. Admittedly it was a lonely prescription, an Rx that might better have been replaced by a 100mg of whatever tricyclic was cutting edge back in the Seventies. But who knew about such things? Instead I'd hide out in the basement of Elliot Bay or in the top floor of the Athenian and in my sporadic blue notebooks track a reading list—Joyce, Pound, Eliot, et al.—that was really little more than a syllabus for a course on exile. You could probably dismiss this as one of those charming agonies of late adolescence, but let me suggest that it's also a logical first step in developing an aesthetic, a reach toward historical beauty, the desire to join yourself to what has already been appreciated and admired. You want to find your self in the flow of time, miraculously relieved of your irrelevance. For reasons both sensible and suspect folks today are uneasy with the idea of a tradition, but the intellectual luxury of this stance wasn't available to me, and I saw the pursuit of historical beauty, the yearning for those higher essences other people had staked their lives on, as the hope for some kind of voice, a chance to join the chorus. I was mad for relevance, connection, some hint that I was not alone. I started scribbling in notebooks in part just so I'd have an excuse, a reason for sitting where I sat, an alibi for being by myself.

Seattle in the Seventies was the nadir of just everything. A UW Prof. of mine, a yam-faced veteran of SDS, inelegantly labeled us the phlegmatic generation. The word *apathy* got used an awful lot. I quite sincerely believe Karen Ann Quinlan was the decade's sex symbol. Seeking an alchemic dullness in Quaaludes and alcohol she actually found apotheosis in a coma—that's what made her so sexy (i.e., compelling) and symbolic to me. I'm not trying to be ironic or waggish here. Objects restore a measure of silence to the world, and she was, for those ten wordless years, an object. Her speechless plight seemed resonant, Delphic. The reason I remember her as such an emblematic figure is her coma coincided with my own incognizant youth. The Seattle of that time had a distinctly comalike aspect and at night seemed to contain in its great sleepy volume precisely one of everything, one dog a-barking, one car a-cranking, one door a-slamming, and so forth, and then an extravagant, unnecessary amount of nothing. Beaucoup nothing. The kind of expansive, hardly differentiated, foggy, and final nothing you imagine a coma induces. I read the silence as a kind of Nordic parsimony. An act of middle-class thrift. A soporific seeded into the clouds. All the decent dull blockheads were asleep, and you could no more wake them to vivid life than you could KAQ. Being alone at night in Seattle began to seem horrifying, there was just so much nothing and so little of me.

You know how the story goes—I went away, I came back, blah blah. I now see the personal element in all this, the comic note, and I also realize the high European graft doesn't readily take to all American subjects. The predominate mental outlook of people I grew up with depended largely on a gargantuan isolation. When I finally went away I was always careful to tell people I was from Seattle, Washington, afraid they wouldn't know where the city was, which suggests the isolation of the place was permanently lodged in me. Finding myself at last in the warm heart of culture, in New York or Paris or even LA, I returned, like some kind of revanchist, to the cold silent topography I knew best, the landscape of my hurt soul. I first read Raymond Carver because in paging through his second collection at a bookstore I noticed a familiar place name—Wenatchee—and latched on to the work solely based on that simple recognition. Ditto Ken Kesey. And then there was the discovery of Richard Hugo, a great epic namer, who beautifully described himself as "a wrong thing in a right world" and noted the oppressive quiet of the city the way I had, so that it seemed we were brothers, and offered to me a liberating emblem far better suited to my ambitions as a writer than a girl in a coma. These are probably just the humdrum dilemmas any writer encounters, and that I should express any keen pain at the difficulty of finding a subject and a voice is, I realize, kind of carping and obnoxious. It comes with the territory, after all.

Yet it is still some form of familiar silence that I struggle against when I write, something essential about the isolation. As Graham Greene wrote: "At that age one may fall irrevocably in love with failure, and success of any kind loses half its savour before it is experienced." For me the city is still inarticulate and dark and a place I call home because I'm in thrall to failure and to silence—I have a fidelity to it, an allegiance, which presents a strange dislocation now that Seattle's become the Valhalla of so many people's seeking. The idea of it as a locus of economic and scenic and cultural hope baffles me. It a little bit shocks me to realize my nephew and nieces are growing up in a place considered desirable. That will be their idea, rightly. That wasn't my idea at all. Vaguely groping for a diluted tertiary memory, people used to say to me, "I've heard it's nice out there," and I'd say, "Seattle has a really high suicide rate." (I was kind of an awkward conversationalist.) But really I didn't know if it was nice; it never occurred to me to wonder. I'd shyly shrug and mumble out of the conversation, saying I didn't know, it was home. Seattle does have a suicide rate a couple notches above the national average and so does my family, and I guess that earns me the colors of some kind of native. I walk around, I try to check it out, this new world of hope and the good life, but in some part of my head it's forever 1974 and raining and I'm a kid and a man with a shopping cart full of kipped meat clatters down the sidewalk chased with sad enthusiasm by apron-wearing box boys who are really full-grown men recently pink-slipped at Boeing and now scabbing part-time at Safeway.

Today I go in search of an older city, a silent city. Early in the morning the painted signs on the buildings downtown seem to rise away from the brick in a kind of layered pentimento. The light at that hour comes at a certain angle and is gentle and notice-ably slower, and words gradually emerge from the walls. "Your Credit Is Good." "The Best in Raingear." There is a place I can stand on Westlake Avenue and read the fading signs and recognize many of the names of people I grew up with. I've got my own people buried in the ground. I cross the Aurora Bridge and think special thoughts and know my brother's black Wellingtons are buried in the shifting toxic silt at the bottom of Lake Union. That brother's alive, and I thank God for certain kinds of failure. New silences layer over the old. I hope this brief superficial essay hasn't simply circled around a peculiar woundedness. Folks double my age and older often run down a conversation tracking a vanishing world that will, with the passing of their memory, vanish entirely. This is something more than benign senescent forgetfulness. So be it. Nowadays I feel like an old-timer in terms of estrangement. I don't know what determines meaning in the city any better than these old people with their attenuating memories. Probably traffic laws, the way we still agree to agree on the denotation of stop signs. I went away and in my absence other things have sprung up. Good things. It's a new place, but there's an old silence bothering me.

Now when I write I feel the silence pressuring the words just like the silence I felt as a kid, walking around town, with nowhere to go. It used to be I'd wander down the alley around the corner from the Yankee Peddler and see if Floyd the Flowerman was in his shack. FF sold flowers out of a homemade shack, a lean-to patched together out of realtor's sandwich boards and such and propped up against what's now a soap shop, and he was a big fan of police scanners, of the mysteries of other people's misfortunes as they cackled over the airwaves and received, at least briefly, a specific locus, a definite coordinate within the city. This oddball interest in fixing the detailed location of pain and disaster fascinated me. I'd say it prefigured the job of a writer, if the conceit weren't so obviously tidy. I can't now tell if Floyd was crazy. Probably he was just Sixties jetsam, tossed overboard by the era and living like a kind of alley cat Brautigan "made lonely and strange by that Pacific Northwest of so many years ago, that dark rainy land. . . ." That wet black alley, and then the queer miracle of his white shack, those floodlit plaster buckets filled with red gladiolus, sunflowers, pink carnations, and then Floyd the hippie holdover tuning his scanner into instances of tragedy, dialing up meaning and its shifting vectors. One night when the bus just wouldn't come Floyd and I walked in the rain down Stone Way to watch a house burn. He was very hepped up. The cold rain on our faces warmed to tear-temperature in the heat of the burning house. I wish time would collapse so that I could be watching flames and ash rise from that house and also see my brother falling through the air below the bridge. Obscurely I know this is a wish that Time, like a god, might visit us all in our moment of need. But Floyd's gone, and that brother's got a metal plate in his pelvis and walks a little funny, and myself, I wander around at night, taking long walks to clear my head before sitting down in front of my typewriter, walking for an hour or two as all the new and desirable good floats before me like things in a dream, out of reach, and I peer through the windows of new restaurants and new shops and see all the new people, but I don't go in, probably because I feel more in my element as the man who is out there standing in the rain or just passing by on his way home to write.

Notes on Contributors

T. CORAGHESSAN BOYLE received his MFA. from the Writers' Workshop and his PhD from the English Department at the University of Iowa. He is the author of twelve books of fiction, the most recent of which are *Riven Rock* and *T.C. Boyle Stories*, both published in 1998 by Viking. He is a professor of English at USC in Los Angeles.

ETHAN CANIN is a physician and the author of four books, most recently *The Palace Thief* and *For Kings and Planets*. He is now on the faculty of the Iowa Writers' Workshop.

JUSTIN CRONIN is the author of *A Short History of the Long Ball*, which won the 1990 National Novella Award, and a collection of linked stories, *Mary and O'Neil: A Romance*, forthcoming from The Dial Press. A graduate of Harvard University and the Iowa Writers' Workshop, he is an associate professor of English and writer-in-residence at La Salle University in Philadelphia.

CHARLES D'AMBROSIO is the author of *The Point and Other Stories*. His new novel, *Train I Ride*, will be published by Knopf. He lives in Seattle.

STUART DYBEK is the author of three books, and his poetry, fiction, and nonfiction have appeared in numerous magazines and anthologies. He was a Teaching Writing Fellow at the University of Iowa in 1973 and a guest teacher in 1998. He has been the recipient of a 1998 Lannan Award, the PEN/Malamud Prize, a Whiting Writers Award, a Guggenheim Fellowship, and two NEA fellowships. Currently, he teaches at Western Michigan University.

DEBORAH EISENBERG's last collection of short fiction is *All Around Atlantis*.

TOM GRIMES is the author of three novels, *A Stone of the Heart, Season's End,* and *City of God;* a play, *Spec;* and a historical fiction anthology on the Iowa Writers' Workshop. He directs the MFA Program in Creative Writing at Southwest Texas State University.

DORIS GRUMBACH is the author of seven novels, five memoirs, and a biography. Working very slowly on a fourteenth book, she lives a secluded life with a beloved friend of twenty-five years on a quiet cove with no visible neighbors. She is eighty.

BARRY HANNAH, a Mississippian, has taught at Montana, Iowa, Middlebury, and has been writer in residence at the University of Mississippi since 1983. He has authored eleven books of fiction and has been honored by the American Academy of Art and Letters, the editors of *Esquire* magazine, and the Guggenheim Foundation. In April 1999, he was awarded the Chubb-Robert Penn Warren Prize for Fiction from the Fellowship of Southern Writers.

JAMES HYNES is the author of a novel, *The Wild Colonial Boy,* and a book of novellas, *Publish and Perish: Three Tales of Tenure and Terror.*

WILLIAM LASHNER is a graduate of both the Iowa Writers' Workshop and the New York University School of Law. As a trial attorney in the Department of Justice's Criminal Division during the Reagan Administration he worked in the Narcotic and Dangerous Drug Section as well as the Office of Special Investigations, which is the government's Nazi-hunting unit. The rights to his novels *Hostile Witness* and *Veritas* have been sold worldwide, and the works have been translated into ten foreign languages. He currently lives outside Philadelphia with his wife and three children, where he writes full-time.

FRED G. LEEBRON's novels include *Out West* and *Six Figures.* His stories appear frequently in magazines such as *Grand Street, TriQuarterly, Ploughshares, Threepenny Review,* and *North American Review.* He is co-editor of *Postmodern American Fiction: A Norton Anthology* and co-author of *Creating Fiction: A Writer's Companion.*

MARGOT LIVESEY grew up in Scotland and now lives between Boston and London. She is the author of *Criminals* and *Homework* (novels) and *Learning by Heart* (stories). Her new novel, *The Missing World,* will be published early in 2000.

ELIZABETH McCRACKEN's first collection of stories, *Here's Your Hat What's Your Hurry,* was an American Library Association Notable Book of 1993. Her novel, *The Giant's House,* was a finalist for the 1996 National Book Award. She has won grants and awards from the American Academy of Arts and Letters, the Guggenheim Foundation, the National Endowment for the Arts, the Michener Foundation, and the Fine Arts Work Center in Provincetown.

JAMES ALAN McPHERSON is the author of *Crabcakes, Hue and Cry, Railroad,* and *Elbow Room,* for which he won a Pulitzer Prize in 1978. He is currently a professor of English at the Iowa Writers' Workshop.

CHRIS OFFUTT is the author of two books of short stories, *Kentucky Straight* and *Out of the Woods.* He has published a novel, *The Good Brother,* and a memoir, *The Same River Twice.* His work is widely anthologized and has received many honors, including a Guggenheim Fellowship and a Whiting Award. He was recently commissioned as a Kentucky Colonel.

JAYNE ANNE PHILLIPS is the author of two novels, *Shelter* and *Machine Dreams,* and two widely anthologized collections of stories, *Fast Lanes* and *Black Tickets.* She is the recipient of a Guggenheim Fellowship, two National Endowment for the Arts Fellowships, a Bunting Institute Fellowship, and a National Book Critics Circle Award nomination. She was awarded the Sue Kaufman Prize in 1980 and an Academy Award in Literature in 1997 by the American Academy and Institute of Arts and Letters.

SUSAN POWER is the author of *The Grass Dancer,* winner of the 1995 PEN/Hemingway Award. She is a graduate of Harvard College, Harvard Law School, and the Iowa Writers' Workshop, and the recipient of a James Michener Fellowship, Radcliffe Bunting Institute Fellowship, and Princeton Hodder Fellowship. Her second novel, *War Bundles,* will be released in 1999. She currently resides in St. Paul, Minnesota.

FRANCINE PROSE is the author of nine novels, two story collections, and most recently a collection of novellas, *Guided Tours of Hell.* Her stories and essays have appeared in *The Atlantic Monthly, Harper's, Best American Short Stories, The New Yorker,* the *New York*

Times, The New York Observer, and numerous other publications. She writes regularly on art for *The Wall Street Journal.*

MARILYNNE ROBINSON is the author of the novel *Housekeeping.* Her second novel, *Mother Country,* was a finalist for the National Book Award for nonfiction in 1989. She lives in Iowa City, where she has taught at the University of Iowa for seven years. In 1998 she received a Mildred and Harold Strauss Living Award from the American Academy of Arts and Letters.

SCOTT SPENCER is the author of seven novels, including *Endless Love, Waking the Dead, Men in Black,* and *The Rich Man's Table.*

ABRAHAM VERGHESE, MD, is a professor of medicine at Texas Tech University Health Sciences Center and a 1991 graduate of the Iowa Writers' Workshop. He is the author of two books, *My Own Country* and *The Tennis Partner.* His work has appeared in *The New Yorker, Granta,* and other publications. He lives with his wife and three children in El Paso, Texas.

GEOFFREY WOLFF has written six novels, most recently *The Age of Consent.* At work on a life of John O'Hara, he has also published biographies of Harry Crosby *(Black Sun)* and of Wolff's father *(The Duke of Deception),* together with a collection of personal essays, *A Day at the Beach.* He directs the MFA fiction program in writing at the University of California, Irvine.